PhilanthropyRoundtable

Excellent Educators

A Wise Giver's Guide to Cultivating Great Teachers and Principals

Laura Vanderkam

Karl Zinsmeister, series editor

Current Wise Giver's Guides from The Philanthropy Roundtable

Karl Zinsmeister, *series editor*

For all current and future titles, visit PhilanthropyRoundtable.org/guidebook

TABLE OF CONTENTS

PREFACE

The Human Heart of Great Schooling

Research demonstrates that the most important factor in the success or failure of a school is its teachers. The intelligence, skill, and dedication of the instructors overwhelms factors like the amount of money spent, or the quality of the facilities. If you want to improve schools, you have to improve the general level of teaching. And degrees and credentials—as you're about to learn—have little to do with teacher excellence.

Principals, meanwhile, are the people who select teachers. They guide and assess and train and dismiss them, throughout the year, and over their careers. Without bold, wise, and sober leadership a school is unlikely to build more than a middling set of instructors.

The central role of teachers and principals in educational success is why we have created this book for donors. It offers concrete, research-proven advice on how to bolster those two professional positions. We steer philanthropists to the factors that can really make a difference, and dispel many myths and misunderstandings floating about in this arena.

The Philanthropy Roundtable gratefully acknowledges the generous assistance of the Rainwater Charitable Foundation in supporting the publication of this guidebook.

Whatever your philanthropic priorities, we hope you will consider joining The Philanthropy Roundtable. You will enter a network of hundreds of top donors from across the country who share lessons learned and debate the best future strategies. We offer intellectually challenging and solicitation-free meetings, customized resources, consulting, and private seminars for our members, all at no charge.

For more information, please contact any of us at (202) 822-8333 or K-12@PhilanthropyRoundtable.org

Adam Meyerson, president, The Philanthropy Roundtable
Dan Fishman, director of K–12 education programs
Anthony Pienta, deputy director of K–12 education programs

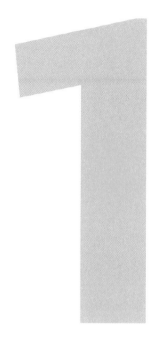

Good Teaching Trumps All

Brett Pangburn's sixth-grade English class at Excel Academy in East Boston is a pleasant enough place. There's nothing particularly striking about it at first glance. Student work decorates the wall. The classroom is neat, orderly, and welcoming.

But linger in the back of the classroom for a minute and you soon start to see extraordinary things. On a mid-September morning, just a few weeks into the school year, none of these preteens stare out the window at the row houses defining the area. None of them seem to be mentally transporting themselves anywhere else. Instead, the sixth graders track their English teacher as he moves around the classroom—the whole classroom—gliding between desks as if he owns the place. This possession of the classroom's physical space is all the more interesting given that at Excel, a charter school serving primarily Latino and lower-income children, the teachers change classrooms between periods, not the students. Pangburn has just walked into the class a few minutes before; the kids have been here all morning. Still, the classroom is his, and two dozen sets of eyes stay on him as he discusses language clues.

Pangburn asks one child for the answer to a multiple-choice question. The child answers correctly. Pangburn nods—and then he ups the classroom engagement level by pivoting to another child to ask a fol-

Great teaching can close achievement gaps.
That's why smart philanthropists are so
anxious to make teachers more effective.

low-up question on why the other multiple-choice options weren't right. The girl's hand wasn't raised, but it doesn't matter, because in Pangburn's class, everyone will be called on. Everyone has to think. That's what great teaching ensures.

As a middle-school tutor years earlier, Pangburn recounts in an interview, he discovered that his first preteen charges "seemed like really bright kids. But they didn't know anything. The work they were doing was a joke. You think, huh, these kids sound really bored. They're not being challenged."

While student-teaching at dysfunctional Boston schools, he likewise observed that "there were issues. But in my mind the issues weren't with the kids. It was the adults in front of them."

After transitioning to teaching from a legal career, Pangburn "humbly accepted that I didn't know what I was doing. I tried to figure out who's good and go watch them." After observing expert teachers, he'd try their techniques. Then he'd have these expert teachers come watch his class.

"It's about being reflective," he says. "I'm hungry for feedback." If something doesn't go well, he wants to fix it.

Excel students show up with various disadvantages. More than half speak a language other than English at home. Only 16 percent of their parents have pursued any education beyond high school. About a quarter of the children receive special-education services. More than two thirds of Excel's fifth graders arrive reading three or more years below grade level.

Yet by seventh grade, the year after many of these students have had Pangburn, 100 percent will score proficient or advanced on the English-language section of Massachusetts' state test. This is all the more remarkable given that Massachusetts has one of the harder achievement exams in the country. Excel students' advanced and proficient ratings means they can truly compete with the rest of the world.

Great teaching can close achievement gaps. That's why smart philanthropists are so anxious to make teachers more effective. As Sid Richardson Foundation president Pete Geren puts it, "the three most important factors in quality education today are, number one teachers, number two teachers, and number three teachers."

Changing the quality of education often becomes a question of who. Who is in front of our children, working to stretch their brains? How do these people get there? And how do they get better at what they do?

Of course, great teaching cannot succeed in a vacuum. Excel is a high-performing charter school with a strong school culture. Pangburn recalls walking in for the first time and seeing that the students "were smiling, and nobody was yelling." Better yet? "The adults in the room clearly thought the children could do rigorous work, and were helping them to do that work, and pushing them to do that work. I was blown away, and thought this is the kind of place I want to be."

There are teachers with the capacity to be excellent in schools around the country. These teachers work hard to challenge their students, only to see their work undermined in some cases by ineffective teachers in subsequent years. They see their precious planning periods eaten up by pointless meetings and paperwork. Getting master instructors and mentors in to offer helpful feedback and coaching isn't part of the culture. Colleagues don't share lesson plans and collaborate to meet student needs. And they lack the data to know how they're doing.

Good teaching can exist on its own, but great teaching requires great systems. And great systems are often about school leadership—principals who no longer see their jobs as managing a building and following district rules, but as nurturers of human talent, with a hard-nosed focus on operational excellence. Great school leaders can turn intelligent and hard-working teachers into educators who change the trajectory of children's lives.

Not for love or money

There's no doubt that many children's life trajectories need changing. Philanthropists who work for educational excellence quickly learn that one reason powerful schools are so important is because children from impoverished circumstances often deal with bleak conditions in the rest of their lives. If schools don't set high expectations, and train children in habits of study and discipline, and help them dream of a bigger life, many children will grow up without these things.

We have a long way to go. In Philadelphia, for instance, the public schools recently celebrated that 61 percent of students who began high school in 2008 graduated on time in 2012. This was the first year in ages that the number had surpassed 60 percent.

That's common in urban areas across the country, despite massive spending in the educational sector. The U.S. spends far above the industrial-nation average on primary and secondary education. Our average spending per pupil rose from about $2,835 in the early 1960s (in 2009-2010 dollars) to well over $13,000 now. In Newark, New Jersey, a district that graduates fewer than 70 percent of its students on time, the figure is at least $17,000 by conservative measures, and $24,000 by other calculations. Much of the increase in per-pupil funding across the country stems from the billions districts have spent keeping class sizes small. But small class sizes don't help if the teachers are mediocre. Many parents would actually prefer a larger class with an amazing teacher over a smaller class with a subpar instructor.

What's more important than money, we've learned, is the quality of the educators working in schools. "People focused on transformative solutions realize that human capital has to be improved," says Richard Barth, CEO of the KIPP Foundation. "There is no workaround to the challenge of attracting, selecting, developing, and advancing" top teachers and principals.

No doubt the vast majority of people who choose to work in education do so because they love and care about children. Caring is great, but caring by itself is insufficient. Teacher and principal quality is as much about tools and strategies as it is about how much people care. Coaxing high performance from children is a skill, and like all skills it can be taught, practiced, and improved over time.

So how can that be achieved? How can philanthropic investment help bring about a world where every child has a string of great teachers—not an occasional lucky assignment, but a reliable relay of good instruction every year, with each teacher building on the work of the last? How can donors help make sure that teachers are nurtured and held accountable by school leaders with a commitment to excellence, and the management skills to make their vision a reality?

There are organizations applying new approaches to teacher and principal recruitment, training, retention, and evaluation today, generally thanks to philanthropic support. These innovators bring more untraditional teachers like ex-lawyer Brett Pangburn into the classroom. They train teachers in practical methods like the roaming and questioning techniques Pangburn uses. They use classroom video recording and

> The key is to focus on what helps
> children, not on what is most convenient
> for teachers and principals.

online instruction to hone instructional skills. They score and mentor and re-train teachers who are already in the classroom to help them improve, and sometimes adjust their salaries accordingly. A few dozen cities and states have let go of tenure in an effort to improve teaching.

In all these things, the key is to focus on what helps children, not on what is most convenient for teachers and principals. Good schools put children first, and find educators with the same priorities. And when this happens, new horizons open. "Before Excel, I didn't think about my future," recalls one student in an essay posted on Mr. Pangburn's wall. "But now I do, because I know I want my dream job."

Wise giving involves taking risks that others won't, and it requires some patience. Leo Linbeck III, a Houston area businessman and philanthropist, notes that "It's taken a long time to get into this mess. We're not going to get out of it overnight."

Wise giving also means learning from others' experiments, so money isn't wasted. Donors need to know what peers have tried, what they're excited about, and what hasn't worked as well as intended. "If it's not moving the needle on student achievement, it's not worth a long-term investment," says Lisa Daggs, chief program officer of the Doris and Donald Fisher Fund. This guidebook will help you make those kinds of practical investments—in teachers and principals who can change lives.

What Quality Is and Why It Matters

Looking back on their own time in school, most people can recall extraordinary teachers. They can usually recall some lousy ones as well. Yet experts have often tied themselves in knots trying to define an effective teacher.

Somewhere between the meaningless credentials demanded by box-checking bureaucracies and the crude common-sense standard we sometimes feel in our guts ("I know one when I see one"), there are hard indicators we can refer to. If the goal of a school system is to create educated citizens, then for years Chicago Public Schools have been badly staffed. In 2011, only 21 percent of Chicago eighth graders were proficient or better on national reading standards, and only 20 percent were proficient or better at math.[1] Yet under their longstanding rating system, 93 percent of Chicago teachers earned "superior" or "excellent" ratings.[2] This defies common sense. Says Howard Paley, chief operating officer of the Rodel Foundation: "If students are not learning in class, that teacher can't be considered a great teacher." As a former educator himself, he notes that the job is not just about showing up and delivering material. "Our job is to ensure students learn."

The traditional approach to defining and rewarding teaching quality, however, hasn't looked at whether students are learning. Instead, districts have generally looked at input factors. Inputs are easy to see and measure. So most states put a heavy emphasis on teachers being certified. Prospective teachers generally become certified by studying at an approved university's school of education. But a teacher's performance, never mind the performance of his students, turns out to have little connection to whether a certificate was obtained.

Districts generally compensate teachers based on years of experience. This is easy to measure, and almost all teachers improve during their first few years on the job. But then many level off—yet continue to earn pay increases as they age. Veteran teachers can easily be earning twice as much as entry-level teachers[3] (well into six figures, in larger districts), though there's no evidence they achieve twice the results.

Many districts also define a high-quality teacher as one who has a master's degree. Districts in the U.S. spent about $15 billion in additional compensation for master's degrees in the 2007-2008 school year, though in most subjects there is no link between a graduate degree and student achievement. The funds tied up in master's degree bonuses represent money that can't be used for other things. Automatic compensation for master's degrees amounted to $446 per pupil in Illinois, for instance, in

---

1. nces.ed.gov/nationsreportcard/districts

2. ccsr.uchicago.edu/sites/default/files/publications/Teacher%20Eval%20Report%20FINAL.pdf

3. See Newark's salary scale, for instance, here: ntuaft.com/Info_Center/Forms/teacher-clerk_contract.pdf, p. 58-60

2007-2008. That could cover 20 hours of individual tutoring, or the cost of a tablet computer, for every single student.[4]

According to studies, one of the few inputs that might matter is a teacher's own academic skills, as assessed by college grades, standardized test scores, and the selectivity of college attended.[5] [6] These are proxies for intelligence. As Jessica Lahey, a teacher who blogs for the *New York Times*, puts it, "I think a lot of it comes down to being able to think really fast on your feet." The children aren't grasping your original approach, so can you improvise another way of reaching the same objective? Some states require a test of basic competence for teacher certification, but the bar isn't particularly high.

The reality is that most current systems for accrediting and paying teachers make no meaningful distinctions between good instructors and poor ones. An important 2009 report called "The Widget Effect," published by TNTP, used data to illustrate how teachers are effectively

> Almost all teachers are rated good or great by today's ranking systems. Less than 1 percent of teachers receive unsatisfactory ratings—even in schools where students fail to meet basic academic standards year after year.

treated as interchangeable units by school districts today, rather than as individual talents. Almost all teachers are rated good or great by today's ranking systems. Less than 1 percent of teachers, the report showed, receive unsatisfactory ratings at present—even in schools where students fail to meet basic academic standards year after year.[7]

As a result, excellence goes unrecognized. When everyone is given top ratings, truly exceptional teachers cannot be identified. Nor can they be compensated, promoted, or retained. In this environment, few teachers develop as professionals as fully as they should. In their last evaluation,

4. americanprogress.org/issues/education/report/2012/07/17/11934/the-sheepskin-effect-and-student-achievement

5. dartmouth.edu/~dstaiger/Papers/w14485.pdf

6. nsf.gov/statistics/seind02/c1/c1s5.htm

7. widgeteffect.org

almost three out of four U.S. teachers received no specific feedback on improving their performance. Novice teachers are also being neglected. Low expectations and a toothless tenure process mean that beginning teachers receive neither prods nor support that push them toward excellence. And perhaps worst of all, poor performance goes unaddressed. Half of the districts studied had not dismissed a single tenured teacher for poor performance in the previous five years. None dismissed more than a handful each year. Students suffer grievously from the failure of our schools to differentiate among teachers, and no significant improvements in teacher quality are likely to take place until more honest and accurate systems of assessment and advancement are put into place.

Figuring out teacher quality is worth the trouble

So our public education system has generally rewarded inputs that don't matter, and ignored the few that might. This is frustrating, given how much teacher quality matters. A growing research consensus finds that teacher quality (of which principal quality plays a part—a story we'll get to later in this guidebook) is the most important school variable in student achievement. It is more important than factors that school authorities obsess over (and pour huge amounts of money into, over recent years) like class size.

Economist Eric Hanushek of Stanford University has studied teacher effectiveness for more years and in more depth than any other academic today. He recently made a simple calculation: What if we stopped arguing over what it is that makes some teachers effective and simply accept the reality that certain instructors are more effective at getting students to produce test scores? His results are powerful.

Replacing the least effective 7-12 percent of all teachers with teachers who are merely average "would bring the United States to the level of the highest-performing countries in the world, such as Finland."[8] This would in turn have an energizing effect on our economy, as children whose brains had been somewhat more fully stretched applied their skills to solving national problems. Approaching Finland's educational achievement would, "by the historical patterns of economic growth, yield a gain in present value of more than $100 trillion over 80 years," according to Hanushek.

That chunk of change is surely worth the trouble of figuring out more accurate measures of teacher quality—and then acting on what

---

8. Hanushek, Eric A., "Education Quality and Economic Growth," in *The 4% Solution: Unleashing the Economic Growth America Needs*, Bush Institute, 2012, pp. 226-239.

we discover. Fortunately, in the past few years, education has seen a great expansion of the available metrics—in many cases spearheaded by philanthropy. Improved ways of measuring are starting to change what we know about teacher quality, moving the definition away from crude inputs and gut feelings to something more accurate and rigorous.

One of the most intriguing changes is the growth in value-added tests. The Measures of Academic Progress (MAP) exam, which is now a staple of charter schools and used by a growing number of conventional district schools as well, assesses students at the beginning and end of the year. Because it is a computerized assessment, the MAP is able to adjust to each student. Whether a child is advanced, average, or lagging, the test will give a fine-grained measure of what she knows, and what she's learned over the course of her time with a particular teacher.

These cumulations of how much new knowledge a child absorbs during a school year are referred to as "value added." When you look at an entire classroom of students and determine how far they move during a school year from where they started, you have a very relevant and valuable measure of a teacher's effectiveness. Technology is enabling a culture of more accurate and timely assessment. Schools that work with the Achievement Network, for instance, a nonprofit supported by the Michael & Susan Dell Foundation, the Walton Family Foundation, and other donors, get valuable data and assessments on the progress of their students every 6-8 weeks. They are taught how to value this data and use it to improve student instruction.

There is often wide variance in what different instructors achieve. Teachers in the top 20-25 percent of the distribution can produce 1.5 years of academic gains in a year; those in the bottom 20-25 percent average only half a year's student progress during a school year. In other words, the effective teachers produce literally three times the gains of ineffective teachers.

Picture two children who start first grade with the exact same academic skills. One is assigned to three top teachers in a row. He or she would start fourth grade with the knowledge of a mid-year fifth grader—a level that would qualify the child for gifted programs in some schools. Meanwhile, a similar child subjected to three low-quality teachers in a row would be performing like a second grader as he or she entered fourth grade.

For children who start school behind their peers, even average teachers (those in the 25th to 75th percentile, who produce about a year of gains in a year of time) will leave them behind the pack. Only excellent teachers can close achievement gaps. The first crucial step, therefore, is to use value-added tests to reveal which teachers obtain superior, average, and poor results with their students.

Teaching must be taught

Once you know who achieves greater student growth, you can work backward to try to understand and improve performances. What do superior teachers do differently? Are there common techniques and approaches that let them take children from all walks of life and move them forward toward rigorous standards?

Doug Lemov and Uncommon Schools have become famous in education circles over the last few years for their study of this question. Uncommon Schools—a network of high-performing charter schools in Newark, Boston, Brooklyn, and elsewhere—systematically evaluated its best-performing teachers to study their methods. Lemov's team analyzed hours of videotape—as football coaches might do—to see how teachers kept students engaged, on task, and thinking hard. Lemov's resulting 2010 book, *Teach Like a Champion*, isolated 49 specific skills that excellent teachers use. Among them:

> *They "cold call" on students.* The old tradition of hand raising is ingrained in schools, but why should only children who want to be called on get engaged? In one video clip on Lemov's site, second-grade teacher Hannah Lofthus cold calls on the same girl twice in a row.[9] The point is clear: I control this class, and you'd better pay attention.
>
> *They circulate.* Moving around the room forces children to pay attention, and keeps people in the back from disengaging.
>
> *They narrate positive behavior.* ("I see Daniel thinking. Carlos made a reasonable guess...").
>
> *They make maximum use of classroom time.* Losing just five minutes a day in paper shuffling or cajoling children to gather in a circle wastes 15 hours in the course of a school year.
>
> *They stretch students to add depth to their answers.* Requiring students to take their thoughts one step further cements and extends understanding.

---

9. teachlikeachampion.com/the-classroom

Rather than presenting predigested information, they pull kids into the process of instruction. Great teachers know that they're in a different line of work than preachers and motivational speakers. They avoid straight lectures and make their kids do much of the cognitive work in class.

They plan lessons intensively—not only what they'll do, but what the students will do. Teachers prepared for things that could come up are able to make interesting diversions even as the original objectives get met. Planning doesn't squash spontaneity, it enables it.

Lemov found that these techniques and dozens of others he has identified correspond with student gains. He and Uncommon Schools have now instructed more than 10,000 teachers on how to use them. They will train the teacher-trainers of any interested district. In about a dozen workshops per year, Lemov reports, "we do a two-day overview of some part of the content (classroom culture; reading; high academic expectations; pacing; etc.). We model what training looks like and make them experience it as participants. Then they step back and reflect on how to use and adapt these things in their setting. They leave with 50-75 videos and an electronic binder of ready-to-use materials so they can lead workshops for teachers in their own districts." Funders have given grants to school districts and charter operators so they can go through this program.

Another very important effort to bring research rigor to the question of what good teaching looks like is the Measures of Effective Teaching project spearheaded by the Bill & Melinda Gates Foundation. Researchers studied 3,000 teachers in cities including Charlotte, Memphis, and Pittsburgh. They used student surveys and student gains on achievement tests. They relied on multiple trained observers to assess educators on how they managed behavior, created a culture of respect, engaged students in learning, and other factors. These measures were combined to create an overall measure of effectiveness for each teacher.

For children who start school behind their peers, even average teachers will leave them behind the pack. Only excellent teachers can close achievement gaps.

Then researchers assigned the teachers to new classrooms to see if their MET scores would accurately predict how effective they would be with a different, randomly assigned group of students. They did. The study concluded that "it is possible to identify great teaching by combining three types of measures: classroom observations, student surveys, and student achievement gains."

Improving teaching requires work

Clearly, these methods could be invaluable to schools serious about improving their teaching. At the same time, hard results like these can be threatening to some incumbent teachers. To try to soften resistance to scientific assessments, the MET researchers noted that their system can be used to improve feedback and support, as well as for sorting instructors. "While some teachers' low performance will require administrative action on behalf of students," the measures also "provide rich information to help teachers improve their practice…. Many of the teachers who participated in the MET project video study told us that seeing themselves teach was one of their most valuable professional development experiences."[10]

The Gates Foundation is now focusing many of its grants around MET principles: "It's a big thing for us," says program officer Ebony Lee. "A lot of what we do over the next couple of years will look at what systems can do to accelerate implementation of those." How can districts get hiring and compensation right? How can they build professional development that can help instructors improve? Most schools are just beginning to "hold teachers accountable and give them data that has consequences," says Lee. And "some places are more hostile to change than others."

It should be encouraging to see that the crucial elements of effective teaching are for the most part skills that can be learned. If teachers were "good" or "bad" based on some inherent qualities of personality, then options for improving performance would be limited. Ineffective teachers would be reduced to keeping their heads down and just hanging on until retirement. All school leaders could do would be to try to fire poor teachers, which can be almost impossible in school districts governed by union agreements. But if good teaching is a skill, then this opens up more positive prospects, if parties will commit to making necessary improvements. Skills can be learned and practiced, even if you've already been on the job for a while.

---

10. metproject.org/downloads/MET_Feedback%20for%20Better%20Teaching_Principles%20Paper.pdf

As economists like Eric Hanushek have shown (see the beginning of this chapter), removing the bottom 10 percent of teachers would be a big win for the students who'd otherwise be consigned to their classes. It would also give an upward jolt to the productivity of the country as a whole. But it won't overcome today's shortage of excellent teachers. We don't just need to get rid of bad teachers; we need a significantly larger number of good teachers. It is good teachers who will overcome the achievement gap at the bottom of our schools.

Larger numbers of effective teachers should be developed in the same way that talent is created in other sectors. Recruit from pools of smart people, train them intensely in practical skills, hire carefully, conduct careful ongoing observation and measurement of results, offer feedback and practice for improvement, reward success, and point those who remain ineffective toward some different career. "Teaching isn't that different than lots of other fields," says Norm Atkins, founder of the Relay Graduate School of Education.

"People are beginning to rethink the staffing model of schools in a way that could dramatically improve the education kids are getting, and also transform the profession into something that's much more attractive to high caliber people," says educational researcher Bryan Hassel. The next chapter looks at how good teachers can be recruited, trained, retained, and evaluated, so that quality isn't just a side effect of extraordinary personal initiative, but is built into our educational structures and incentives in a way that leads to consistent results.

Reinforcing
Teacher Quality

Great teaching can look deceptively easy. Nadirah
Sulayman, for instance, is relaxed and friendly as
ninth-grade English students enter her class at a
Mastery charter school in West Philadelphia. There is
no hint of tension over the breadth of material she is

about to cover. Yet during the next 50 minutes she takes her students on a dizzying whirl of reading comprehension skills: a quick assessment of a previous assignment, an introductory tour of a new book, a few minutes of silent reading, some group work, and a chance to test their mettle on a difficult passage (more on that later).

She picks her battles with an eye on the larger goal. A student mumbling a question to a seatmate about something in a book is fine—it's part of figuring out the text—whereas another student answering a question with her hand in front of her mouth is given a swift reminder: "Hand!" She creates an atmosphere that is both orderly and expansive.

She moves through the whole room to figure out what students are thinking. "I've learned the power of circulation," she says, remembering the first classes she faced as a Teach For America corps member ten years earlier. "I used to think the teacher had to be up front." Part of what kept her stuck up there is that "I was still leading so much of the lesson." In her decade of teaching she's learned to make students rely on her less, and use their brains more.

Toward the end of the class, Sulayman passes out a copy of Liam O'Flaherty's classic short story of civil strife in 1920s Ireland, *The Sniper*. It's part of an exercise she calls "structured struggle." The students read the first few paragraphs. They start annotating—tricky words they don't recognize, what they think is happening, what is unclear. She pairs the students up and they compare notes on the opening:

> The long June twilight faded into night. Dublin lay enveloped in darkness but for the dim light of the moon that shone through fleecy clouds, casting a pale light as of approaching dawn over the streets and the dark waters of the Liffey. Around the beleaguered Four Courts the heavy guns roared. Here and there through the city, machine guns and rifles broke the silence of the night, spasmodically, like dogs barking on lone farms. Republicans and Free Staters were waging civil war.

The children in this class were born long after the IRA had fallen out of the news headlines. "Republican" is a word they know, but incorrectly as it is used here. And Dublin? As Sulayman circles the class she deduces that a reasonable proportion of the student pairs think Dublin is a person, perhaps the name of the sniper. That might make the story a placeless dystopian tale, which is a fascinating idea, though not what O'Flaherty intended.

Sulayman is perfectly fine with debating wrong ideas. From what she observes while walking around the class she chooses three interpretations of what's going on. Then she has students argue over them. The goal? Developing strategies for figuring out something you are unfamiliar with, and learning to weigh whether an idea is right or wrong without someone telling you.

Sulayman learned early on to put examples of student work up on the board. In the beginning, she reports, she'd put up the good examples. "Now I put up erroneous work," she says, because everyone can learn from the mistakes. As a side benefit, it helps students to see that everyone makes mistakes. She once wrote an essay on the fly, up on the projector, fixing words and changing sentences while the class watched in order to demonstrate that writing doesn't emerge in perfect form, that knowledge and communication are constructed in messy ways.

Before this campus became part of the well-regarded Mastery network, which specializes in turning around dysfunctional schools (with strong support from philanthropists), fights raged frequently. Students urinated in squirt guns and sprayed administrators. "It was a really unsafe, unproductive institution," says Sulayman.

She herself grew up nearby, but one neighborhood over, where she was able to get a better education. Then she went to Morgan State University. She has been happy to work in a functional school in her home town. But her interest is not in just making school safe. She wants to raise standards.

"English in school has been so much dumbed down over time," she says. "I'm glad we're moving back in the direction of things being tougher." She wants these students to go to college, and knows that when they get there no one will hold their hands as they face difficult work. Figuring out how to learn, how to struggle, how to know when you're wrong, how not to quit—if she can teach her students these things they will be able to succeed on many levels.

Recruiting teachers outside the old channels

Schools need many more teachers like Sulayman. But the cultivation of new teachers today is in many ways a haphazard process. There are few entities devoted to systematically surveying talent, identifying people who'd be great instructors, attracting them, poaching them from competing career tracks if necessary, and then training them to mastery.

Charter schools attract excellent teachers

By Karl Zinsmeister

During the latest decade, a higher quality of candidate has begun to be drawn into the teaching profession. Driving this has been the rising demand for smart teachers from charter schools (which are approaching 7,000 in number, and expanding every year by an additional 600 schools). The growth of alternative recruiting networks like Teach For America is also feeding the upgrade.

For two generations, teachers have lagged other professionals in academic qualifications. To test if this is still the case, in the Winter 2014 issue of *Education Next* Dan Goldhaber and Joe Walch compared the SAT scores of college graduates going into teaching versus other fields. While in 2001 teachers ranked 3-7 percentile points below classmates headed for other kinds of work, by 2009 they were 2-3 points *above* non-teachers. Still not academic stars, but trending in the right direction.

There is good research showing that the individuals hired to teach in charter schools are more likely to be graduates of selective colleges than teachers in conventional schools. A 2004 paper from the Education Policy Center at Michigan State University compared a weighted mix of 20,000 teachers at conventional and charter schools, and found that the charter teachers were significantly more likely to have graduated from a college that *Barron's Profiles of American Colleges* placed in one of their three most selective categories, and less likely to come out of a non-selective or less-selective college.

A 2009 paper by Steven Wilson zeroed in on charter schools that get good results from low-income children and found that 77-83 percent of their teachers came from one of *Barron's* three top categories. (And about two thirds of those came out of a college in the very highest category.) Among teachers in conventional schools, only 19-25 percent graduated from colleges rated in those same selective categories.

While "charter schools face disadvantages in areas like lacking access to funding for buildings, and getting lower per-pupil reimbursements from states," notes Gretchen Crosby Sims of the Chicago-based Joyce Foundation, "they also have great advantages. One of the biggest ones is greater flexibility in deploying their teachers."

Lots of organizations are working to create more good teachers to staff charter schools. Teach For America, which recruits top college graduates and young professionals to teach for at least two years in schools serving needy populations, has moved aggressively into the charter realm in the past several years. Many big urban school districts are losing students and laying off teachers, making it harder for TFA to place its corps members in conventional schools. But the blossoming of charter schools has more than picked up the slack.

In Chicago during the 2013-2014 school year, 59 percent of TFA teachers were working in charter schools. In Philadelphia, an even larger fraction work in charters— only 21 out of 257 corps members taught in conventional public schools in that city in 2013. Nationwide, about two thirds of all TFA teachers work in conventional district schools, but the fastest growing niche for TFAers is charter schools.

Despite these successes, many charters—like most other schools today—don't have as

many truly impressive teachers and teacher candidates as they would like. "The 'no excuses' charter schools depend on highly talented people," says Rick Hess of the American Enterprise Institute, and "staffing all the new schools...while also replacing teachers who retire, fail, or burn out, will be a strain in the future. It will only become manageable if we find innovative new ways to effectively train top teachers, reduce unnecessary burdens on them, and incentivize them to stay with education as a career."

—This is excerpted from the new Philanthropy Roundtable book **From Promising to Proven: A Wise Giver's Guide to Expanding on the Success of Charter Schools,** by Karl Zinsmeister, published in March 2014. See "Chapter 4: Bringing Top Teachers and Principals to Charters."

Contrast this selection process with, say, basketball, where scouts hover and a tall kid with good aim will be told constantly that he'd make a fine player. Compare teacher training with law or business or engineering, where tough classes and stern qualifying exams keep professional standards high.

Or, to look more specifically at an alternate way of producing teachers, consider Finland. Finnish teachers enjoy a great deal of respect, have wide professional autonomy, and get great results on international comparisons. And in Finland, admission to teacher training programs is extremely demanding and competitive. Wanting to be a teacher is absolutely no guarantee that you'll get to become one.

Teachers in Finland have the same profile as individuals accepted into Teach For America in this country: only top students from excellent colleges get in. Imagine if the U.S. teaching corps was all built from Teach For America-caliber raw material, and that these recruits were then trained more extensively than TFA does? That's Finland.

The Teach For America analogy is worth thinking through. Today's most effective alternative teacher recruitment program (and the one that trained Nadirah Sulayman), TFA is a direct product of philanthropic support, built on major and sustained donations from stalwarts like the Doris and Donald Fisher Fund, the Walton Family Foundation, the Laura and John Arnold Foundation, and many others. Founder Wendy Kopp's original vision was that if you started with bright people, most would learn quickly to solve whatever problems they encountered in their classrooms.

Ann Best, TFA's senior vice president of education leadership, notes that when she went through the program in 1996, reading through a binder of key articles was the major part of her training. Since then, the program has learned that its members can do even more if they're more fully trained (more on that later in this section). But Kopp's basic insight was well founded. Recall that studies show teacher intelligence to be more closely correlated with the success of students than other factors.

And TFA recruits are indeed bright. Some 18 percent of recent graduating classes at Harvard have applied for the program, and only about 20-25 percent of these were accepted.[1] From TFA's overall application pool, the rate of acceptance is about half that. TFA also actively recruits retirees looking at encore careers, veterans transitioning out of service, and other experienced or talented populations.

---

1. thecrimson.com/article/2011/9/29/tfa-harvard-students-education

These are people who were not attracted by the conventional routes into classrooms—only 15 percent of TFA corps members say they would have considered a teaching career outside of the TFA system. And there is good research demonstrating the effectiveness of TFA's unconventional teachers. A 2013 study found that TFA corps members teaching math in secondary schools helped their students achieve 2.6 months of additional learning gains compared to the average teacher at their same school.[2]

There are other donor-supported programs that recruit smart teachers not reached by our conventional teacher colleges. Some of these specifically cultivate candidates to fill the hardest staff roles, like math and science teachers for secondary schools (many of whom have other professional options), or special-ed instructors. The Carnegie Corporation's "100kIn10" project, for instance, aims to bolster the ranks of U.S. math and science teachers by 100,000 individuals before 2021.

"We need mathematicians to work at hedge funds, and as medical researchers, and as engineers designing bridges," says Talia Milgrom-Elcott, the coordinator of the program. "I'd never go head to head with any of that. But there's no long-term play for anyone if we're not training more kids to be capable of doing math and science. We only get that if we have more teachers."

The campaign says it has recruited 35,000 math and science educators so far. This project is a ready-made way for funders to invest in teacher recruiting without having to build their own program. A funding commitment of $500,000 over three years is typical. Funders include Carnegie, the S. D. Bechtel, Jr. Foundation, the Michael & Susan Dell Foundation, Google, the Noyce Foundation, NewSchools Venture Fund, and others.

Many of the regional programs participating in the 100kIn10 effort are worth considering on their own as partners in training science and math teachers. For instance, UTeach, founded at the University of Texas at Austin in 1997, helps science and math majors earn their teaching certification while they're studying for their B.S. Now replicated at more than 30 universities across the country, UTeach ensures that technically inclined students get hands-on, practical training in schools, and do internships in nonprofits with science and math emphases. UTeach also provides support during its graduates' first years in the classroom, and according to figures from the group, about 72 percent of its early grad-

---

2. teachforamerica.org/sites/default/files/hsac_final_rpt_9_2013.pdf

The Catholic TFA

America's urban Catholic schools play a key part in the larger cause of educational excellence. While such schools were originally created to teach Catholic doctrine along with the three Rs to parishioners' children, they now provide an escape valve for many non-Catholic kids who would otherwise be trapped in failing public schools, which is why many donors such as the Connelly Foundation in Philadelphia now enthusiastically support Catholic schools. For a much lower cost than the public schools, Catholic schools send a higher percentage of their students to college.

But as with public schools, Catholic schools face challenges in acquiring the talent they need. Religious orders no longer supply significant numbers of teachers. To help fill the gap, the Alliance for Catholic Education was founded at the University of Notre Dame with funding from the William E. Simon Foundation, the Walton Family Foundation, the Bradley Foundation, and others. The program recruits hundreds of bright young college graduates— from Notre Dame's graduating classes, 12 partner universities, and other colleges—to work in needy Catholic schools around the country. These graduates take classes over the summer, teach while living together in communal houses for mutual support, return to campus for more classes, and teach again. Certifications, specialty training in areas like bilingual education, and master's degrees are available to participants in the two-year program.

Since its founding, Notre Dame's ACE program has trained more than 2,000 teachers and leaders, of whom 75 percent are still in education. Schools in over 74 dioceses and archdioceses receive ACE teachers.[1] And close to 300 students now enter the sister programs run by other colleges like Boston College and Loyola Marymount University.

---

1. ace.nd.edu/annual-report

uates were still in the classroom five years later, an impressive retention statistic for science and math teachers.[3]

Of course, it isn't just in technical fields that American schools need better teachers. Finding instructors with detailed content knowledge, and then helping them acquire the practical tools needed for teaching, would elevate the quality of instruction in many fields of K-12 education. That's one reason a number of organizations have grown up to help career changers.

TNTP (founded as "The New Teacher Project") started out helping schools to recruit, train, and hire new teachers with a special emphasis on hard-to-fill specialties like special-ed and math. By locating, training, and certifying non-traditional candidates, its TNTP Academy has been responsible for completing nearly 3,000 tough teacher hires. These teachers have proven to be substantially more effective, on average, than other teachers in similar schools.

> Finding instructors with detailed content knowledge first, and then helping them acquire the practical tools needed for teaching, would elevate the quality of instruction in many fields of K-12 education.

Since 2000, TNTP has also operated a Teaching Fellows program that seeks out accomplished professionals and recent college graduates who weren't schooled or certified as educators but have subject knowledge and talents to help high-need students. The program is extremely selective—only 8 percent of all applicants make it to the classroom. Here again, recruits are particularly steered into the hardest-to-fill jobs: about 40 percent of TNTP Teaching Fellows go into special education, 15 percent teach science, 12 percent teach math, and 10 percent work in bilingual education. More than 32,000 unusually effective teachers have come out of the program since its creation.

The promise of training and a job placement can be a good lure to teaching programs, especially in a tepid economy. The Academy for Urban School Leadership (AUSL) in Chicago, for instance, attracts

---

3. uteach-institute.org/replicating-uteach

150 new teachers to Chicago each year with its yearlong teacher residency. Candidates earn a reasonable stipend while working under a master instructor, and upon graduation these new teachers are employed in schools in Chicago.

Many other similar small-scale programs exist for cultivating new teachers. There remains ample space, though, for funders to help draw additional talented individuals into teaching. Other cities, for instance, could benefit from a pipeline like Chicago's AUSL.

Interest in recruiting talented mid-career professionals into the ranks of teaching has increased in recent years. Teacher certification often poses an enormous barrier to entry, though, keeping capable individuals out of the classroom. Why give up a good job to spend years in a lackluster and expensive preparation program needed for the state credential, only to come out on the other end just marginally more prepared to be an effective teacher? Alternative credentialing pathways are thus especially important for mid-career job changers.

Institutions such as the American Board for Certification of Teacher Excellence were developed to provide an entry-level classroom credential that could be earned online part-time by a busy professional while he or she continues to work. Contrary to criticisms from the teacher-training establishment, 2007 research by Mathematica found that ABCTE's assessments are as rigorous as conventional assessments, if not more rigorous. The ABCTE credential offers school districts a valuable opportunity to bring new talent into schools, because while some charter schools are free to hire widely, nearly all district schools are required to find teachers with credentials. As of this writing, ABCTE is fully state approved in Arizona, Florida, Idaho, Mississippi, Missouri, New Hampshire, Oklahoma, Pennsylvania, South Carolina, Tennessee, and Utah.

Training

After recruiting teachers, you need to instruct, mold, and hone them. Most teachers today are trained at traditional schools of education. Enrollees generally major in educational theory rather than in a specific content area, and these programs have historically not been very selective.[4] Prospective education majors had an average verbal SAT score of 486 and math score of 488 (out of 800) on one recent survey. On those

---

4. See, for instance, studies by Ballou (1996), Vance and Schlechty (1982), the Education Policy Center at Michigan State University (2004), and McKinsey (2010).

same SATs, high-school students who indicated they wanted to study engineering scored 529 and 579 respectively, while architecture students scored 495 and 527.[5] There's some recent evidence that scores are trending up slightly for prospective teachers, but education programs have a reputation as undemanding compared to other professions.

Some of the reasons for this are financial. "The lower the standards you have, the more people you can admit," says Kate Walsh of the National Council on Teacher Quality, who has been studying schools of education for years. She also finds that "There is a very strong anti-intellectual bent on the part of education schools. You hear a lot of people say we need people who really care about kids"—rather than people who are, first and foremost, highly intelligent and hard working.

To raise teaching quality, union president Randi Weingarten of the American Federation of Teachers recently proposed a bar exam for teachers, which would presumably be taken after years of study as happens with lawyers. "The problem with that is you're telling people who've spent years being educated that they can't get into the profession they've just trained for," says Walsh. "It's much more effective to do it at the entry point."

Much of the course work at today's education schools is about how and why children learn, and the role of public education in society. This can be fascinating material, but it doesn't much help a teacher walking into a class of 20 third graders know what she should do Monday morning to keep them engaged. Teacher colleges "don't believe it is their job to train," says Walsh. "If teachers need a tool kit to manage a classroom, that's frowned upon. It's frowned upon that the institution would teach an approach to reading"—as opposed to guiding teachers to develop their own philosophy of reading instruction.

Student teaching, meanwhile, tends to be limited. Few colleges provide much oversight of the feedback and technique-training that student teachers get, and few programs ensure that students will be assigned to master teachers who get results. A former principal recounts an instructor asking for a student teacher because she had so little control of her class she needed a second adult present to mitigate the chaos.

A few organizations are looking at upgrading student teaching. The Rodel Foundation of Arizona, for instance, recruits (and pays) highly effective teachers to take student teachers under their wings. They

---

5. nces.ed.gov/programs/digest/d05/tables/dt05_128.asp

recruit master instructors who view it as part of their own professional development to train a new generation. Master teachers must agree to take on six student teachers over a three to four year period.

Because teacher-college training and student teaching is generally so ineffective, most starting teachers are not effective. For students, "the learning loss under first-year teachers is striking and measurable," says NCTQ's Walsh. "We've come to accept a system in the U.S. that says the first year is trial by fire. We don't think that's necessary. We think we've settled for far less than we could expect."

Schools of education are hardly monolithic. The NCTQ gives high marks to Vanderbilt University and Ohio State University, to the University of Central Florida, and the University of Maryland at College Park, among others. Funders concerned about the lack of rigor and wisdom in most teacher preparation could try to reorient more teacher colleges. But redirecting an institution of higher education is notoriously difficult, and disappointed donors are legion. The Lynch Foundation, for instance, worked to establish a new program for training principals at the Lynch School of Education at Boston College. The foundation became discouraged the university was identifying very conventional leaders for what they felt should be a fresh approach.

"Very candidly, we struggled to create an innovative program in a traditional university culture," says Katie Everett, the foundation's executive director. They wound up working instead with Boston College's Carroll School of Management, which was more receptive to their notions of how principal training needed to be improved. (See the next chapter for more on the Lynch Leadership Academy.)

Can traditional schools of education be fixed?
While new alternative programs for recruiting, training, and certifying teachers have proliferated across the country (excellent examples are profiled below), donors can't ignore traditional schools of education. As Sid Richardson Foundation president Pete Geren puts it, they "are important because they're enormous. Each year, schools of education put over 200,000 individuals into the teacher pipeline—that's 80 percent of all our new teachers."

In 2013 the National Council on Teacher Quality published an exhaustive multi-year review of 1,130 of the nation's teacher-prep programs. Many of the schools reviewed had never been thoroughly assessed in areas like student-selection criteria, subject-area preparation of graduates, practice-teaching experience, and classroom outcomes. The results were jarring. Only four programs out of these 1,130 earned a top rating of four stars. Fewer than 10 percent of the programs earned at least three stars.[6] The disaggregated data tell an even starker story:

- Three quarters of U.S. teacher-prep programs accept students who rank in the bottom half of their high-school class. (The countries with top educational results only accept the top third of students into their teacher programs.)
- Only one out of every nine elementary-education programs gave teachers sufficient content expertise to successfully teach the new Common Core state standards.
- Fully 75 percent of elementary-preparation programs don't teach the most effective, successful methods of reading instruction. Often, they encourage untested teacher candidates to develop their "own unique approach" to teaching reading.
- Only 7 percent of programs had protections in place to ensure that student teachers were placed in classrooms with effective instructors, rather than just someone who wanted the help of a student teacher.

Rigorous practice teaching in a classroom, a skill that all new instructors need from day one, is insufficient at nearly all conventional teacher programs. And schools of education are not required to track the performance of graduates and report back on the effectiveness of specific candidates, or the preparation program as a whole.

Numerous donors, some chronicled in this guidebook, have worked to improve traditional teacher preparation programs, but this is a difficult fight. Teacher-prep is a $7 billion annual business, and a financial bonanza for many of the colleges and universities that house these programs. Unlike a chemistry major, for example, where each student requires expensive investments in equipment, supplies, and instruction, the costs for adding additional candidates to teacher-training programs are low. There's no incentive for these programs to look for new ways of doing business.

Nor do outsiders wield many carrots or sticks that can be used to improve teacher-prep. The lack of meaningful accountability allows

---

6. nctq.org/dmsStage/Teacher_Prep_Review_2013_Report

schools of education to languish without repercussions. Few universities hold these departments to high standards, and the agencies that accredit them are staffed by individuals aligned with traditional schools of ed. Worst, the "consumers" of the output of these programs—schools and school districts—do almost nothing to demand better prepared teachers. As shown in the "Widget Effect" report cited earlier, districts have failed in their own annual assessments and internal advancement systems even to acknowledge that teacher quality varies meaningfully from individual to individual. So they have left themselves little room to insist on, or even identify, a better quality of teaching candidate.

Tragically, opportunities to be much choosier abound. Teacher colleges have been dramatically overproducing graduates in recent years. Illinois trained 9,982 new teachers in 2011, though the state estimated it only needed 1,073 new teachers. New York overshot demand for new teachers by nearly 3,700 graduates. This bounty of available teach-

Teacher-prep is a $7 billion annual business, and a financial bonanza for many of the colleges and universities that house these mediocre programs.

ers means districts could be much more selective in who they hire, and which preparation programs they hire from. When she was a partner at the NewSchools Venture Fund, Julie Mikuta focused on identifying the best teacher colleges, hoping to encourage "a marketplace in which new teachers who come from programs with a track record of effectiveness are ones who are able to get the jobs." That is how top charter schools now hire, but it's almost unheard of in school districts.

There are a few positive glimmers in this area. The Sanford Education Project at Arizona State University may be one. Philanthropist Denny Sanford put up almost $19 million over a five-year period to launch SEP in 2010 as a distinct program within the university's teachers college. SEP was intended to be different from day one: the program didn't wait for teacher candidates to apply to ASU, it actively sought out excellent teacher candidates from Arizona high schools.

A "major component" of the program, states former director Andrea Pursley, was "building a predictive admissions and progression model.... When we accept a student, what do we need to know about him to know that he is likely to have a dramatically positive impact on student learning in his first year of teaching? What do we need to know at the end of the freshman year, sophomore year, junior year, before student teaching, during student teaching, to be able to predict the success of that teacher as measured by student achievement gains?"

Once carefully chosen recruits entered SEP, they followed a model rooted in Teach For America's proven practices. This included an emphasis on the use of data to assess student achievement and drive student gains. It involved constant practice at actual teaching, with feedback and improvement through videotaped lessons and expert classroom observations.

For a time, SEP represented the cutting edge of teacher preparation, by embedding in mainstream higher education the hard-won discoveries TFA had made during 20 years of struggle and improvement. Unfortunately, this program was eventually resisted by the more traditional teachers college that surrounded it at Arizona State. SEP changed leadership and discontinued some of its practices in response, and has since been renamed the Sanford Inspire Program. While TFA continues a partnership, it's unclear if the current incarnation of this project holds as much promise as SEP. This example thus serves as both a hopeful and a cautionary tale for donors seeking to reshape conventional teacher colleges.

There are a few other rays of hope. When David Andrews, formerly the head of Ohio State's well-regarded college of education, took the helm of Johns Hopkins University's school of education he promised meaningful reform. One reason Andrews made the jump: the faculty at JHU did not hold tenure, a rare circumstance that he hopes will allow him to attract more entrepreneurial faculty who share his vision for moving the program toward a focus on student outcomes. TFA has a partnership with the Hopkins program, which creates programs specifically for TFA students. And unlike any other mainstream teacher college, Andrews and the Hopkins program are moving toward folding hard measures of the effectiveness of teacher candidates (the classroom progress of their students) into their progress, and even into the performance reviews of their professors. While the university has a long way to go in translating these principles into concrete steps in the degree program, these are dramatic departures from teacher-college conventions.

Teach For America as an alternative

Because most education schools have proven so resistant to change, many funders have concentrated on creating alternate ways of getting smart and dedicated instructors into classrooms—like Teach For America. TFA training for new instructors has long centered on its summer institute, but over the years additional and improved instruction has been added throughout the two-year commitment of each TFA participant. "We see the institute as one piece of a broader training and support continuum," says TFA vice president Michael Aronson.

Before their summer training programs begin, corps members complete a high volume of independent and online exercises. Then they spend a week in the region where they'll be teaching, learning about the local context. Next they attend the five weeks of intensive training at the institute. Each teacher undergoes additional training during her first eight weeks at her assigned school year. She participates in frequent individual coaching sessions throughout her two-year commitment. In addition, each school and district offers programming and support for new teachers. The majority of TFA corps members, according to Aronson, also pursue master's degrees while they are in the program.

As TFA studies its most effective corps members, their summer institutes are constantly evolving. In addition to the nine regional summer institutes it operates, in 2013 TFA experimented with locally run institutes in two cities—Memphis and Jacksonville. The idea was to "further customize and tailor our training to the local context," says Aronson. The intent is to get teachers informed on and invested in the history and culture of their particular community. The organization was pleased enough with the outcomes that it will expand this pilot to six cities in the summer of 2014.

Another change involves zeroing in on subject content. "Five years ago, very few corps members were trained in the specific content areas they'd be teaching in the fall," Aronson says. The instruction was in general teaching technique. But the new thinking is that "Teachers need to know their content. So we're invested heavily in content-specific training, from early-childhood information for our pre-K folks to mathematics instruction for secondary-school teachers. We're going to continue to invest in content pedagogy. It's critical."

A third large area where TFA's training has been enhanced is to make it more hands-on. "We're continuing to invest and put energy into making sure that the teaching experience in the summer is authentic and resembles the type of experience corps members will have in the fall," Aronson says. The bulk of a corps member's time at the institute is devoted to student teaching, and TFA is making a point of inviting more kids into the summer-school classes where its teachers practice, so teachers can garner experience with both the subject and the grade level they'll be handling later.

Finally, TFA is gradually rolling out across its regions a powerful in-class system for critiquing and advising members as they instruct children. TFA and the Center for Transformative Teacher Training have collaborated on what is called the Real Time Teacher Coaching model. It allows new teachers to receive steady individual feedback from master coaches (sometimes immediately via earbud) on how they can improve their performance. Together, all of these elements offer an intense training experience for TFA's rookie teachers.

> Teach For America brings in a new flow of talent that wasn't there before, and serves as a seedbed for future education leaders and reformers.

TFA spends $47,000 per corps member over three years for training.[7] (The teacher's salary is paid by the institution employing her.) More than 90 percent of TFAers return for their second year in the classroom (a better rate than other novice teachers). About 60 percent extend their service for at least a third year. Does the investment of $47,000 to bring a bright and dedicated but inexperienced young teacher into a classroom for two or three years make sense as a philanthropic investment?

Many donors seem to think so. The Mind Trust, for instance, helped raise the $2 million necessary to attract TFA to Indianapolis a few years ago. "We concluded that if we didn't have TFA in Indianapolis, our ability to have the talent we needed to do a whole range of things in education reform wasn't going to be there," says the Mind Trust's David Harris.

TFA has become a catalyst for education reform broadly. About a third of TFA alumni remain in the classroom for the long haul, and about

---

7. teachforamerica.org/our-organization/faq

another third remain in education as consultants, education-technology entrepreneurs, at education nonprofits, and so forth. The program thus serves as a seedbed for future education leaders and reformers. "TFA is bringing in this new pipeline of talent in the community that wasn't there before," is how Harris summarizes what he has seen in Indianapolis. If these overflow effects are added to the teaching work of the corps members, the effect per dollar invested is higher.

Relay Graduate School of Education

A number of new organizations are learning from TFA, and seeing if it's possible to attract the same caliber of people TFA gets, systematically train them, and employ them over longer periods of time to take education to the next level. That's what's happening at the Relay Graduate School of Education. The first new teacher training school to open in New York City in 80 years, Relay offers a profoundly practical classroom-proven style of instruction, and it offers official certification—though only to teachers who prove they are effective, as measured in the performance of their students. All Relay enrollees are working teachers, generally coming in through alternative certification programs such as TFA, the NYC Teaching Fellows, TNTP, or as new hires at charter schools. Like any program aimed at working professionals, classes are held on nights, weekends, and online. The purpose is teaching strategies that teachers can take into school the next day.

On a Thursday night in September, a mostly 20-something crowd—racially diverse but predominantly female—gathers in Relay's Chelsea neighborhood New York City classroom space. Professor Mayme Hostetter is teaching the concept of academic rigor. The students review sample lesson plans and discuss which are the most rigorous, which could be better.

These teachers in training give their highest marks to a project looking at hurricane preparation in Florida. Students will study the coastline and population projections, and make recommendations. Then everyone goes to work on his own rigorous lesson plan.

Brent Smart is part of the class. He was born in Barbados, and works as a teaching assistant at Voice Charter School in Queens in NYC. He went to public schools, and did well enough to get into Skidmore College. Though he graduated from that demanding institution four years later, "at Skidmore I found out I wasn't prepared." As he struggled to keep up with his classmates, he decided to go into teaching to keep other young people from facing this same problem.

As a working educator, he appreciates Relay's focus on classroom management skills. For instance, he has learned the importance of tight transitions. "If you think about how many transitions there are, especially in elementary school, efficient transitions save you a bunch of instructional time." He has learned to "always be thinking ahead, how to move things efficiently to maximize time."

Behavior management is only one component of keeping a classroom humming efficiently, though. Smart reports that he has also been taught strategies to check for understanding. Relay's focus on data analysis is "pretty intense," he says, and the numbers show which students are keeping up and which aren't. "We need to track everything, which is good for me. It gives me a benchmark—how I'm performing, and how I can better help my students."

While he was student teaching, "I saw growth in so many areas, especially in students just learning English.... The instruction I got from Relay—it prepared me to support the students in my class, especially the struggling students."

Perhaps the best evidence of Relay's ability to get teachers to focus on rigor and excellence is the fact that Smart was redoing the lesson plan he had brought to class. After looking at examples the professor passed around, he realized that the lesson he had prepared wasn't good enough. So he was working to make it better, a fact that would certainly help his students the next day.

Relay enrollees are held accountable for outcomes among their students. In order to earn their degree, the students in their classrooms must average at least a full year's worth of academic gains in a year's worth of time. No other teacher college has ever used any real-world measure of success like this so meaningfully.

Relay enjoys wide support today from philanthropies like the Robin Hood, Helmsley, Gates, and Arnold foundations, the Carnegie Corporation of New York, and individual donors like Larry Robbins. The goal is to make the program sustainable on its own. Teachers generally pay for their own master's degrees, and the goal is to make Relay so worthwhile that people will be willing to take out loans to cover the cost. Relay has expanded beyond New York City to New Jersey and New Orleans, and other cities will follow. It's also partnered with Coursera to create an online version of the Relay program.

Match's graduate school of education

Relay is not alone in showing that new and very different schools of education, focused on student performance, can be set up outside today's conventional channels. The San Diego charter school network High Tech High established its own state-approved, degree-granting teachers college. Starting with their own need for a reliable supply of high-quality teachers, especially in math and science, HTH created its own training program, which now turns out graduates who flow into schools across the region. Creating your own teachers college is not a small undertaking, but it is doable.

Taking a page from the medical world, a number of organizations are creating teacher "residencies" that provide candidates with a combination of intensive hands-on training and classroom learning, leading directly to job placement. Match Education operates a string of superb charter schools in the Boston area. Match also has created its own accredited teacher school, which grants a master's degree intriguingly titled the "Master's in Effective Teaching."

Match begins its teacher training by being very selective. "Our admissions rate is in single digits," says CEO Stig Leschly (previously an entrepreneur who founded and sold Exchange.com to Amazon in the late 1990s before turning to education reform). Match accepts about a hundred or so candidates to its graduate program each year out of 1,500 interviewed. "We are selective up front, and we make no bones about it."

These individuals are then rigorously trained in classroom performance and management. "We believe strongly that what's required for entry level teachers is how to teach a basic lesson, how to control the environment. They need to develop automaticity about basic teaching techniques." The goal is to help rookie teachers quickly become competent "in real challenges they will face," says Leschly. "That differs drastically from conventional graduate schools of education, where you ask noble questions, but not in our view the ones that matter in the first 12-18 months."

To hone their automatic problem-solving classroom responses, Match's candidates go through "north of 500 teaching simulations through their first year," says Leschly. To make these lifelike, the test subjects will sometimes "randomly misbehave. They'll walk out unannounced." These things happen in real classrooms, and teachers need to be prepared.

But Match teaches much more than how to keep order. "We spend a lot of time coaching our teachers how to check for understanding," says Leschly. They learn techniques for engaging students throughout a whole class, and for steadily increasing the rigor of the subjects discussed. Prospective teachers go through a natural progression: "They practice moves, they scrimmage, then they get their own classrooms."

Most of Match's teacher trainees hold jobs working as tutors in the Match schools. Individual or small-group tutoring is a key part of Match's philosophy, and Match children get at least two hours daily of such instruction. The schools hire their own tutors, often from the ranks of college grads looking to do something meaningful before graduate school. And they hire a lot of tutors. Match Community Day School alone reports that it spends about $1 million on tutors each year. This level of staffing can be achieved because "we're incredibly frugal on everything other than human beings," says Leschly. "We have tutors and teachers and the photocopying."

Tutors are given clear lesson goals. And they are held accountable for results, in an environment with high overall expectations. The day your author visited, a coordinator was videotaping tutors at work so that techniques could be reviewed later.

About half of Match's tutors enter the school to be trained as teachers. After one year, they get full-time jobs teaching (at Match or elsewhere; there is high demand for their graduates). They continue to take online courses and participate in professional development. But as at Relay, they will only receive their master's degrees after test results demonstrate that their students have made good yearly progress.

TNTP

For funders looking to bring an existing national program to their communities, TNTP gets high marks from other philanthropies. Founded by Michelle Rhee in 1997, TNTP has recruited, trained, and placed tens of thousands of new teachers in multiple states. TNTP runs intense summer training programs for its Teaching Fellows, typically in partnership with a university that can credential the graduates. In Indianapolis, for instance, students train from 7 a.m. to 6 p.m. at Marian University from June through July. Then TNTP provides coaching during the graduates' first years in the classroom, while they are simultaneously completing masters' degrees through Marian.

In other regions like Washington D.C., TNTP operates a TNTP Academy—the organization's own instructing and certifying entity. Students do coursework and training directly through these academies, under the guidance of master teachers. In all cases, final certification requires evidence of effective classroom practice.

As at Relay, High Tech High, and Match, TNTP's training is practical and hands-on. Says president Tim Daly, "We take a skills-first approach." Conventional teacher colleges "teach theory and deeper, broader, conceptual things to new teachers. We believe those things are important, but not to new teachers."

TNTP puts "a huge emphasis on practice." Their training inculcates skills until they are second nature. "How you have kids enter the classroom. How you collect papers. Do stuff without kids present over and over again until they're fluent. That is almost never done in schools of education." These skills give TNTP teachers firm control of their classrooms, so teachers can then focus each day's energy on intense instruction, rather than restoring order.

Like TFA and Match, TNTP is highly selective, taking about 8 percent of applicants. TNTP's typical participant is often a little older and more experienced—typically between the ages of 27 and 35. An analysis that studied TNTP teachers in Louisiana over several years found that, on average, students in their classes advanced five percentage points higher in math than those taught by other teachers.

While most of TNTP's operational funding comes from schools themselves (they pay the organization for each teacher placed, and other services), about 30 percent of the group's support comes from philanthropies. Some donors help TNTP advance its research programs. Other supporters provide the funds that allow the program to enter a new region. The Mind Trust, for instance, brought TNTP to Indianapolis just as it did TFA, to accelerate its larger ed-reform goals in its home area.

The Urban Teacher Center

A regional organization focused on Washington, D.C., and Baltimore, the Urban Teacher Center trains English and math teachers. All of its graduates are dual certified in special education. With more than 15 percent of all students in these two districts qualifying for special-ed services, there is always a demand for such teachers. While UTC has received money from the NewSchools Venture Fund, the Michael & Susan Dell Foun-

Conventional teacher colleges teach theory. We believe those things are important, but not to new teachers. We take a skills-first approach.

dation, and others, it also has a "healthy earned income." The dual certification in particular makes districts willing to share the cost of training and bringing in a UTC teacher.

Like the other alternative teacher trainers we've been profiling, UTC ties its certifications to the teacher's proof of effectiveness. The children UTC instructors work with are often already behind peers. These teachers are expected to prevent them from falling further back by generating at least a year's worth of gains in a year's worth of time. Teachers who can produce more than a year's worth of gains in a year's time are prize resources who can change children's lives. By making sure they are only turning out teachers who get results that reach the national average or above, UTC, Relay, Match, and company are taking the risk out of hiring for schools. In the words of UTC co-founder Christina Hall, "We've cut the bottom half off the bell curve."

These alternative training programs calculate student performance results with painstaking care. TNTP, for instance, mixes standardized tests, expert observations, and student surveys. The resulting scores can be compared to "a universe of other teachers with similar students," notes TNTP's Tim Daly. To be certified, you need to be better than most of your peers. "Have you earned a second year in the classroom? In some cases it's an unambiguous yes. In others, it's a clear no." If a candidate doesn't clearly perform better than an average teacher, "then we part ways." In borderline situations, TNTP will sometimes extend a candidate for a second year without certifying, and make a final decision after one more year of performance data is available. If there isn't clear improvement, that person will be coached out of teaching.

As Daly puts it, "The philosophy we have is that the only excuse for teaching like a beginner is if you are a beginner. A second-year teacher who still teaches like a first-year teacher? We would rather put a new first-year teacher in your place."

This tough front-end selectivity has great value to schools. In many cases, it's difficult to get rid of ineffective teachers after their first years on the job. Once teachers are tenured, they have many job protections, and firing someone for poor performance can be extremely difficult. What Relay, Match, TNTP, UTC, and company are promoting are training methods that allow a school to see whether a person can be an effective teacher or not before they make what is often a permanent decision. "If someone struggles, they tend to persist in their struggle," notes Daly. It's better "to address that in a direct way up front than to remediate that for years and years."

Measure, and then act

Tying teacher certification to classroom efficacy is an important breakthrough. But to do that, you need good data on teacher and student performance. Many organizations are working on accurate measures. "I think it's a really important time," says Doug Lemov of Uncommon Schools. "In the history of innovations, the innovation was always proceeded by advances in data, advances in measurement. We're clearly at that point" with teaching today. "All of a sudden we can measure things like never before."

Many schools now use the Measures of Academic Progress (MAP) comparison that was described near the beginning of Chapter 2. It assesses performance at the beginning of a school year and at the end. A nonprofit called the Achievement Network, often known as ANet, is helping 470 schools in Massachusetts, Illinois, Louisiana, Michigan, New Jersey, New York, Tennessee, and D.C. collect even more detailed information on how students are doing every few weeks. That way, teachers can make mid-course corrections.

The aim, says CEO Mora Segal, is to make it possible for "every teacher in the building to walk into their classroom and see with great clarity what each student needs academically." ANet is supported by national funders such as Gates, Walton, and Dell, and by regional donors in the states where they are working—like the Barr, Lynch Family, Shippy, Flamboyan, Skillman, and Hyde Family foundations.

Today's growing availability of data can give reformers all kinds of insights. That's how TNTP realized that you can know after one year whether someone has the stuff to be an effective teacher. "People used to think of the first year of teaching as a random data point," says Doug Lemov. "It turns out the data is pretty indicative. If you didn't learn to master the classroom environment in the first year, you never really got it."

TNTP also discovered it worked better to bring more people into its training programs, and then weed them out as time passed. That produced a better caliber of teacher than smaller classes more carefully screened in advance. Good measurements are still not as plentiful as could be desired, but the best teacher training programs are using statistics more, both to assess their candidates and to show future teachers how good measurements can help them better understand and instruct their K-12 students.

Frequent, accurate feedback is how people improve. ANet's Segal reports that the schools using their quick-results measures "are improving at about two times the rate of their peer schools," on average.

Workshops vs. evaluations

These new approaches to training teachers are exciting, but they're also relatively small. Between them, TFA and TNTP may have trained about 60,000 teachers, many of whom have the capacity to transform lives. There are 3 million teachers working in the U.S.

Rapid transformations sometimes overtake overpriced industries, which the U.S. college system surely is. It's possible that our system of teacher training could break open if the rest of higher education breaks open as a result of online competition or other changes. But it's also possible we will see business as usual in the mainline teacher colleges for years to come. In the meantime, what about the 50 million kids and 3 million teachers already in the system? What can be done there?

Many of today's 3 million are doing a good job. Even at so-called turnaround schools, where a dysfunctional campus is shut down and restarted with new leadership, and everyone has to apply for their old jobs, the new leaders often keep a few of the old teachers. At Grover Cleveland school in Philadelphia, for instance, which is now part of the Mastery Charter Schools network that employs Nadirah Sulayman, CEO Scott Gordon reports that even in that horribly failing school, 5 percent of the teachers demonstrated an ability to be effective. They were retained, and he says they are now the "happiest" faculty there. Having struggled for years under bad leadership, they appreciate the different system, with different expectations, that they are now part of.

There are some bright spots and energetic people almost everywhere. Most teachers, however, would benefit from better incentives, a better school culture around them, and improved training. So donors need to ask: How can we help teachers with potential improve? How do we keep more of the best people in teaching? How can evaluation, feedback, promotion, and compensation systems be set up to encourage continual school enhancement?

Those questions lead to this question: Can any substantial gains be wrung out of existing structures of so-called "professional development" (PD in ed jargon), the regular institutionalized training that teachers cycle through? PD is already widespread, but varies widely in value. Mora Segal of ANet concludes that "professional development is a billion-dollar industry in education, but it's heavily driven by hiring a local former principal to come in and do a workshop for a day. It doesn't stick."

Many teachers have had bad experiences with professional development and participate grudgingly or with low expectations. As one highly rated teacher interviewed for this book put it, "I would rather have my fingernails pulled out than go to most PD." A recent trend is for districts to invest in coaching, believing that one-on-one training can do what workshops cannot. But again there are no standards here, and no accountability.

Even new ideas have a hard time attracting the attention of jaded teachers. TNTP launched a program called "Great Teaching, Great Feedback" that allows any teacher to upload videos of himself or herself teaching, and get expert feedback. Uptake has been slow. "Teachers rarely do it" without prompting says Tim Daly. "The idea of opening your practice up to others is fairly new. The door has been so closed."

Regular evaluations have become a science at some companies. At the consulting company McKinsey, associates get reviewed every six months, with a designated evaluator calling dozens of people each associate has worked with, resulting in a rating for each person. A high rating leads to big bonuses and promotion. A low rating leads to being told you must work closely with leaders and mentors to improve—or being "counseled to leave." This sort of system keeps quality high and ensures associates have incentives to improve.

Teacher evaluation systems, however, have long been meaningless. The vast majority of teachers get thoroughly positive ratings that don't reflect the huge differences in outcomes between teachers. These broken evaluation systems have profoundly negative effects on retention. When high achievers aren't appropriately recognized and rewarded, they tend to counsel themselves to leave—the exact opposite of what you want to have happen.

In response, some funders are looking at ways of linking teacher evaluations to concrete student results, like the results coming out of the Measures of Effective Teaching system funded by the Gates Foundation. (See page 21.) If student performance, teacher evaluations, and school pay can be aligned together, then incentives for good teaching could improve dramatically.

REACHing in Chicago

Efforts to put some real substance in systems for evaluating existing teachers were nudged forward by the U.S. Department of Education's Race to the Top grant competition. States seeking funds had to at least loosely link teacher evaluations to student outcomes. Some 40 states now include some measure of student achievement in teacher evaluations, and in 20 states it's a substantial connection.

This has occasioned much suspicion and resistance in parts of the educational establishment. Chicago has been trying to reform its evaluation system, with contentious results. Student test scores are only one part of a broader evaluation rubric called REACH, which touts feedback to teachers and efforts to help them improve. Teachers would be observed multiple times by administrators and experts, and coached on what they could do better. Nonetheless, the modest use of student test data in teacher evaluations was one of the factors contributing to the strike that the teachers union launched at the start of the 2012-2013 school year.

Even though REACH bases only a quarter of a teacher's evaluation on student test scores, the vast majority of Chicago teachers said they believed this was too much. Some of this may have been due to poor explanations of exactly what kind of student scores would be involved. One teacher told the researchers funded by the Joyce Foundation to evaluate the effort that "I can't stop gang violence. I can't stop poverty. I can't stop the parents who don't care if their kids go to school....Those are things that a teacher cannot possibly control." But "value-added scoring" removes much of this problem by looking not at absolute results but rather at each student's progress from his starting point.

Despite resistance, change is in the air. People are quibbling about how to hold teachers accountable. But the conversation is not about whether teachers should be held accountable.

A teacher of bright kids in a suburban school who begin at the 95th percentile and end the year at the 95th percentile will not score well on these rubrics. However, a value-added testing system will strongly reward a teacher in a tough school whose students come in among, say, the bottom 5 percent and end the year at the 20th percentile. That teacher has done a good deal to advance her charges, and she will be rewarded for that, not punished, even though they remain far below average. The only teachers who have reason to fear value-added testing are those who don't see their students improve while they are in their classrooms.

The evaluations of REACH showed that some principals clearly didn't buy in either. They insisted that they already knew who was effective and who was not. In a district in which a great many students are clearly failing, principals were more likely than expert evaluators to give out top scores to teachers. In fact, hardly any teachers got unsatisfactory ratings from principals. And these subjective evaluations are weighted far more heavily than test performance.

"It remains to be seen whether or not REACH will work," says Butch Trusty, former director of education programs at the Joyce Foundation. If only 2-3 percent of teachers receive unsatisfactory ratings, can the other 97 percent at least be given a sense of where they could get better? "If you are able to provide teachers and principals with more nuanced data about their performance, it could enable all sorts of other decisions that affect quality in the system." Despite all the resistance, there seems to be change in the air, notes Trusty. "People are quibbling about exactly how to hold teachers accountable for student results. But the conversation is not about whether teachers should be held accountable."

IMPACT in Washington, D.C.
The move toward meaningful annual evaluations of teacher performance has gone much further in Washington D.C. That's largely thanks to a group of major philanthropists including the Walton, Robertson, Arnold, and Broad foundations. To get a pathbreaking deal arranged, they put $60 million of financial sweetener into the pot to increase pay for teachers, which helped convince the Washington Teachers Union to withhold objections.

Under the district's new IMPACT system, half of a teacher's evaluation score now comes from how much students improved their standardized test scores after a year in her classroom. Other measures of increased student achievement, plus five classroom observations by principals and master teachers, are also used to grade teachers.

Instructors in D.C. whose value-added score shows them to be "highly effective" get a cash bonus of up to $27,000. Two "highly effective" ratings in a row lead to a salary raise of as much as $25,000. Getting repeated "highly effective" scores yields the equivalent of about a five-year jump on the standard teacher salary scale. As you might expect, this resulted in higher rates of retention by the district of excellent teachers.

On the other hand, Washington teachers who get reviewed as "ineffective" are subject to dismissal, as are those rated "minimally effective" for two straight years, and those scoring for three years in a row at the middling level of "developing." During the first couple years of the new assessment system, 500 teachers with poor ratings for effectiveness were let go from the D.C. Public Schools.

Washington's assessment system offers coaching and other help for poor and middling performers to improve their classroom practice. Because the coaches have the detailed performance reviews to work from, they can personalize the professional help needed by each teacher, rather than offering general training like typical teacher-development seminars.

The first major academic assessment of D.C.'s new system of teacher evaluation, done by James Wyckoff of the University of Virginia and Thomas Dee of Stanford, was released late in 2013. It showed that a rigorous value-added approach to grading teachers has clear positive effects in both retaining good teachers and pushing out persistently ineffective ones. Teachers at the margins were incentivized to use the professional assistance—those with one low rating sought help to avoid a second, and those near the top of the middle rating made efforts to become "highly effective."

When supporting performance-pay systems, donors should ensure that teacher evaluators are skilled and well-trained, and that evaluations use clear criteria. Evaluations should be transparent, with no mystery to make teachers nervous or feed any fair grievance. All agree that these evaluations should drive toward teacher improvement, not just punitive action. Donors might help reduce resistance to value-added assessments by financing the inclusion of teacher input in the creation of evaluation documents, and by funding assistance from experts who have established well-regarded teacher evaluation systems elsewhere. The Harrison School District of Colorado, for example, has been heralded for having developed an effective teacher-evaluation and performance-pay system that both teachers and administrators support.

Keeping good teachers

Once you know for sure who your effective teachers are, you want to make sure these good teachers stay. According to the National Commission on Teaching and America's Future, 50 percent of all teachers leave their job within a five-year period. The New Teacher Center has been working on improving this statistic for years, with funding from the William and Flora Hewlett Foundation, the AVI CHAI Foundation, and others. The organization currently works with about 25,000 rookie teachers across the country.

"First of all they're overly optimistic," says CEO Ellen Moir. "That's the nature of starting a new job. They think they're going to be better than they are." In some cases, teachers have seen an outstanding teacher like Nadirah Sulayman make it look easy. Then they get parent complaints, student behavior issues, and lessons that flop. If they're not prepared and resilient, "you feel so deflated." To head this off, the New Teacher Center sends expert teachers into classrooms to coach and mentor new instructors every week.

If you've made the investment in hiring someone and giving that person a classroom, you obviously hope he or she works out. But a key insight in education reform circles over the past few years is that high turnover in and of itself is not necessarily a bad thing. If people figure out teaching isn't for them, better that they move on to something that's a closer match for their skills than stick around and drag down students year after year. You certainly don't want them moving into administration just to get out of the classroom.

The problem is, the people you want to leave teaching aren't necessarily the ones who do. Plenty of wonderful young teachers leave upon having families to do something more lucrative or less stressful. Meanwhile someone across the hall who's pulling down a six-figure salary may just be biding time until retirement. "Good people leave in droves," says Doug Lemov. "Stopping that by honoring them, by training them, by giving them opportunities to shine is the easiest big fix."

In 2012, TNTP produced a report called "The Irreplaceables," which documented the problem of benign neglect. Looking at the top 20 percent of teachers in urban schools—those achieving 5-6 months of additional academic gain among students, compared to lower performers—TNTP found that only 47 percent had actually been told they were high-performing. Perhaps even worse? Only a quarter of the "irreplaceables" reported that someone had identified leadership opportunities for them, and only 37 percent said someone had encouraged them to keep teaching at the school. Almost as many low performers (31 percent) had been encouraged to keep teaching, and a full quarter of low performers had actually been told they were high performing!

The report noted that "principals use retention strategies at similar rates for high and low performers." This is absurd since, according to TNTP, you have only a 1 in 11 shot of replacing a high-performing teacher with someone equally as good. Whereas you have a very good chance of replacing a low performer with someone better.

What would be better ways to keep good teachers? TNTP suggests more feedback, more recognition, more resources, and putting good teachers "in charge of something important." This last idea raises a tricky issue. In many organizations, the way to earn more money and prestige is to move into management. If a great teacher aspires to become a principal and shows talent for managing adults, that may be a good thing. However, many great teachers don't want to manage on a schoolwide level, or aren't equipped for it.

A number of funders are therefore looking at career ladders for teachers that give them more leadership opportunities and expand their influence over more students, without forcing them out of teaching. The Milken Family Foundation has invested heavily in the "TAP" system, which allows teachers who show they are effective to become mentor teachers and then master teachers. Mentor and master teachers become part of the school's leadership team and work with the principal to set learning goals, and they coach other teachers on instructional strategies. A school with 30-40 teachers might have four mentor teachers and two master teachers. Mentor teachers maintain full teaching loads in addition to their leadership roles, and master teachers are in the classroom approximately half the time. Whether in the classroom or not, they work more hours and days, and they are compensated accordingly.

Approximately 400 schools in 10 states use the whole TAP system, and some districts use part of the system. There tends to be more cooperation among teachers when it's one of their own peers providing feedback. Jason Culbertson of the National Institute for Excellence in

Teaching, which oversees TAP, says that when a teacher hears from master teachers, "she knows they didn't just get the strategy off the Internet the night before. They've used it with these students in this building and have evidence of its effectiveness."

A number of other programs are trying to cultivate teacher leaders, and expand their capacity. Leading Educators, a nonprofit that works in New Orleans, Kansas City, Washington, D.C., and other cities, trains teachers to be department chairs and grade-level chairs. It provides the skills necessary to help them coach the teachers who report to them. In addition to creating strong teacher-leaders, Leading Educators allows for a testing of the waters on adult management, which may lead to better principals. Many experts lament that, too often, the first experi-

> When a teacher hears from master teachers, she knows they didn't just get the strategy off the Internet the night before. They've used it and have evidence of its effectiveness.

ence principal candidates have leading adults is when they assume their principalship. Programs like Leading Educators give excellent teachers an opportunity to hone their managerial skills in a role with lower stakes.

Recognizing the need to create better career ladders and growth opportunities to keep talented teachers from leaving education, organizations like Teach Plus help experienced instructors find ways to transform schools and improve school systems. Focused on "second stage" teachers with 2-10 years of experience in the classroom, Teach Plus offers policy fellowships, networking events, and opportunities to voice opinions that may not be heard from union representatives of teachers. The goal is to organize corps of experienced, talented teachers to help turn around failing schools.

Teach Plus Policy Fellows meet monthly for 1.5 years in six cities around the nation with the goal of realizing "tangible, teacher-driven policy impact." In Indianapolis, Memphis, and Boston, for example, local school districts have adopted a number of the policy recommendations that Teach Plus fellows have proposed. The Boston recommendation spawned Teacher Turnaround Teams—groups of effective, experienced teachers who are deployed to failing schools as a body (often ten or more). The idea is that if supported with the right policies, these teams can improve school culture and change student expectations and academic performance.

We could have fewer and better teachers

It's worth noting how fashionable ideas about school staffing have made it harder to keep teacher quality high. A frenetic push for smaller class sizes created a massive expansion of the teacher work force over the last generation. "During the past half-century, while the number of pupils in U.S. schools grew by about 50 percent, the number of teachers nearly tripled," notes Chester Finn of the Thomas Fordham Foundation. "Spending per student rose threefold, too."

Hiring more teachers made unions happy, but it also soaked up money that might otherwise have been used to increase the quality and pay of teachers, Finn notes. "If the teaching force had simply kept pace with enrollments, and school budgets had risen as they did, today's average teacher would earn nearly $100,000, plus generous benefits. We'd have a radically different view of the job, and it would attract different sorts of people."

America invested in more teachers rather than better teachers. "When you employ three million people and you don't pay especially well it's hard to keep a field fully staffed," says Finn. "Especially in locales like rural communities and tough urban schools that aren't too enticing. And especially in subjects like math and science where well-qualified individuals can earn big bucks doing something else."

The most direct way to increase the influence of the best teachers is to be more selective in hiring and then place more children in the classes of excellent instructors. One approach might be to offer a bonus of $1,000 or so for each extra student a proven master teacher agrees to take into her class. This might not work in districts with strict class-size limits or other obstacles in their union agreement. But where teachers and parents opt in, it could magnify the effect of the best teachers. Outside funding might make it easier to put this into effect in a district. Schools might also use technology or teacher's aides to expose more children to top instructors. Researchers at Public Impact recently released a report stating that if schools used these tools, they could pay some teachers at least 20 percent more, in some cases without new funding.[8]

---

8. opportunityculture.org/wp-content/uploads/2013/10/Six_Ways_to_Pay_All_Teachers_More_Within_Budget-Public_Impact.pdf

Some of these changes involve using paraprofessionals to assist teachers in handling larger classes. This has long been standard at colleges, where experts in a field teach large courses, which then have small group discussions led by graduate students. Particularly in areas like secondary math and science, where there is a dearth of qualified teachers, a similar system might use teacher's aides to extend the reach of master instructors.

Blended learning is another way to expand the scope of great teachers. Blended learning combines technology and face-to-face teaching in ways that optimize both. By using technology to deliver basic instruction, teachers are freed up to spend more time working one-on-one with students. Lessons can be instantly differentiated to each child's level of mastery, and students can practice skills like reading and math problem-solving with the instant feedback that helps people improve, instead of enduring the three-day-lag of hand-graded quiz results.

Class sizes in some blended schools reach 30 to 40 kids, or even a 75-to-1 pupil-to-teacher ratio at the Carpe Diem schools. While not for all students, typical students in blended schools perform quite well. They're engaged with personalized lessons online while the teacher works with smaller groups and aides circulate to keep students on task. This substitutes smart machines and lower-priced labor for rarer and more expensive labor, allowing schools to be very selective about who they hire and allowing a great teacher to reach more children.

This is similar to a hospital, where it makes no sense for a surgeon to go around taking temperatures every four hours. A highly-skilled teacher should not be grading spelling worksheets. Another upside is that if you have one teacher for 75 pupils, you can pay her more, and invest more in professional development, sabbaticals, and other skill builders.

A number of charter schools have implemented full-blown blended learning programs. Rocketship Schools, Summit Public Schools, Carpe Diem, KIPP Empower in Los Angeles, and other campuses are starting to see impressive results. KIPP Empower LA has relatively large classes under its blended learning model, but some of the highest scores in the entire KIPP system. In 2013, 95 percent of second graders at the school were proficient or advanced in English language arts, and 98 percent were proficient or advanced in math. Despite its disadvantaged student body, KIPP Empower was the highest-performing school in the Los Angeles Unified School District, and the tenth highest-performing elementary school in all of California." (For more on blended learning, see our sister volume devoted entirely to such schools—*Blended Learning: A Wise Giver's Guide to Supporting Tech-assisted Teaching*.)

Many blended learning schools started in California. In part, that's because the proximity of Silicon Valley makes the use of technology a natural thing. But it's also because California has been in a deep educational funding crisis for years. Blended learning can offer some financial relief by reducing the number of excellent teachers who need to be found.

What about paying good teachers more?

Blended learning can create the space to pay great teachers more. There are also other ways of achieving this, as in Washington, D.C.'s pay-for-performance reform discussed earlier. If top teachers earned more, would we get better quality? What if we somehow raised teacher salaries generally?

> Blended Learning allows schools to be very selective about who they hire, and allows a great teacher to reach more children.

Some experiments offer insights. In New York City, a charter school called TEP ("The Equity Project") launched with a splash a few years ago with its announcement that starting teacher salaries would begin at $125,000. Performance bonuses could add tens of thousands more—putting teaching salaries in line with what some lawyers earn. Would that lead to results?

One school paying outsized salaries might be able to poach educators from nearby campuses in a way that could not be replicated if it was done in all schools. Even ignoring that, the results at TEP were solid but not exceptional. During the school's first few years, as it was expanded by one grade per year (a standard approach with new schools), 8-10 new teachers needed to be hired annually. During the first four years, TEP wound up parting ways with about a quarter of its hires each year. "That's not something we aspire to, that's just the reality," says founder Zeke Vanderhoek.

As TEP worked the kinks out, though, test scores rose, and TEP is now ranked in the top 10 percent of New York City public schools, despite the high poverty of the children attending. However, this charter school doesn't just pay more. All the teachers are "'at-will' employees who have to meet certain expectations, or otherwise they're not retained," says Vanderhoek. And they have to take on more tasks to make the economics work. TEP operates on the same per pupil allocation that other charter schools get. It makes its teachers' higher salaries work by expecting more of them, and employing fewer administrators and support staff.

One teacher doubles as an assistant principal. There is a social worker, but there's no guidance counselor. Teachers run the after-school programs. All this leads to longer hours. One reason some people go into teaching is that the hours are shorter than many other jobs, with summers off. TEP pays teachers like lawyers, but also expects them to work lawyer hours. The result is that TEP sometimes burns people out, as law firms do.

Teacher Dan Vazquez describes a day starting at 7:30 a.m. and running through after-school clubs that conclude around 5:30 p.m. "It is a lot of work," he says. "Yes the salary makes it nice, but at the same time it's a stressful job." A number of his colleagues left because of the hours. On the other hand, he notes, "You want talented people teaching your kids." A funder might help replicate this charter school model in other communities, to see if high-paying and highly accountable schools could attract enough educators, and produce sufficiently strong results with children, to be broadly viable.

Fellowship programs that increase salaries are another way donors have tried to attract better people into teaching. Math for America, partly funded by math-professor-turned-hedge-fund-operator James Simons, pays math and science majors who become teachers an additional stipend beyond their scaled district salary. This stipend can total up to $100,000 spread over 5 years. Conversations with teachers in this program reveal that the fellowship's networking and professional development opportunities are also valued.

A donor interested in other subjects might pay for enrichment for teachers of that topic. Writing teachers might get their tuition paid at summer writing workshops. English teachers could be sent to England to see Shakespeare's plays on his home turf. Summer study and sabbaticals for certain highly effective teachers can give them new perspectives and keep them in the profession longer.

Prizes are another technique certain donors have used to sweeten the financial rewards of teaching. The Milken Educator Award is primarily aimed at teachers fairly early in their careers. Jane Foley, a former Indiana elementary-school principal who runs the program, looks for teachers who show a wide devotion to their profession. They are publishing papers, and presenting at national conferences.

There might be for-profit methods by which top teachers could increase their compensation. Teachers Pay Teachers is an online marketplace where teachers buy other teachers' lesson plans. With thousands of teachers voting with their money, good practitioners rise to the top. This has happened in South Korea, where some teachers build online tutoring businesses to supplement their salaries. That's not attractive to everyone, but it could make teaching more lucrative for entrepreneurial types.

Why school leaders matter for teacher quality

Great performances rarely happen in isolation. Great teachers seek out others who excel, and flee dysfunctional environments. That's why Brett Pangburn from Chapter 1 wound up at Excel, not in the Boston Public School system, and why Nadirah Sulayman works for a Mastery charter school, not one of Philadelphia's traditional institutions.

Dysfunctional environments also prevent teachers who have the potential to bloom from ever progressing beyond mediocre. On the flip side, a dedicated and energetic principal can get more out of almost all teachers. Good school leaders often cycle through classes all the time, observing how things are going, and offering feedback in both casual and formal settings.

"You've got the kids' attention, but I noticed your transitions from one type of work to another aren't as brisk as they could be." "The same three children raised their hands for the questions; maybe you could wait a little longer for more participation, and narrate the wait time to engage more students?" "I'll take your class for this period on Thursday so you can go watch Ms. Brown down the hall."

In schools with a collegial environment where teachers are open to feedback, this can elevate everyone's game. At schools that are successfully closing the achievement gap this kind of thing happens constantly. At the Grover Cleveland charter school in Philadelphia, principal Rashaun Reid reports that he's in teachers' classrooms or meeting with them at least 85 percent of his time. He sets weekly teacher goals, and has worked on improving his own skills at delivering professional advice.

Charter schools have pioneered a different conception of school leadership from the old days, when the principal was often in his or her office dealing with discipline and operational matters. It's not that operational matters don't matter. They do, and principals (or someone) needs to deal with them. Being disciplined about spending, for instance, can allow great leaders to find funds for special projects. But focusing on the quality of teaching is vital if you want great schools. A school leader who can coax better performances from teachers can lift hundreds of students in positive ways.

Jean Desravines, CEO of New Leaders (formerly known as New Leaders for New Schools) says that his organization was started 13 years ago under the premise that "the principal's primary role is to drive student achievement. At the time that was foreign. Most people viewed the principal as the school manager, the disciplinarian, not the person who's the CEO of student achievement gains."

Today's new-style school leader can put "a tremendous focus and emphasis on teacher quality," says Desravines. "What is often missing is appreciation and understanding that the only way you get teacher quality and efficacy on a large scale is through great leadership." The leader is responsible for setting the culture, and for actually finding the instructors and developing them.

In the business world, there's a saying that people join organizations but flee managers. In surveys, teachers name their principal as a primary reason they stay or go. A great leader can keep fine teachers on the job for more years, so they can influence more children. That's why philanthropists interested in the question of teacher quality must also focus on principal quality.

Reinforcing
Principal Quality

By 5:55 a.m., every seat in the classroom of Building
Excellent Schools is taken. The students—who all want
to start their own charter schools—are required to be
at this Boston nonprofit's headquarters at 6. But many
have come earlier. They are clutching their coffee. The
nearby Starbucks, mercifully, opens at 5 a.m.

Instructor Sue Walsh, a veteran educator sometimes called "the principal whisperer," is there to talk through what they're going to see during a long day. First these BES Fellows will visit two high-performing schools. They'll rigorously critique the schools. Then they'll work on the designs of their own proposed schools. Finally, they'll hash out these matters with BES staff until dinner.

Why the sweatshop hours? If you're going to change the world by creating something new, BES founder Linda Brown says, you need to get started before breakfast. Brown originally envisioned her program as something for middle-aged career changers. "That hasn't happened, but I think that's probably good. What this takes is a whole lot of energy and time," she says. So "most of our fellows are under 30. You can't build a school with a family, two dogs, a house, and a station wagon."

The students are mostly former teachers, many with nonprofit or administrative experience, too. They come in clusters from a few regions, including Baton Rouge, Omaha, and Los Angeles, where they intend to open new campuses. Now in its twentieth year, BES has incubated many excellent schools: Democracy Prep in New York, the Excel schools in Boston (where Brett Pangburn teaches), Ivy Prep in Atlanta, Endeavor College Prep in Los Angeles, and lots of others. BES has received funding from the Broad Foundation, the Hyde Family Foundations, and the Walton Family Foundation, among many. Some donors, like Walton, also offer startup grants for BES Fellows' schools.

The BES philosophy is that people who want to start schools should see the best of what's out there, figure out what works, and then try to make an even better institution. It is somewhat jarring at first to hear people criticize schools that are better than what 99 percent of children will ever see. After viewing a young TFA teacher whose class is completely controlled and engaged, the students note that her questions weren't as rigorous as those of a more experienced teacher next door. Walsh is even critiquing the architecture. The building at Excel—where 100 percent of students score proficient or advanced on the state assessment by their third year—is panned for not creating a collegial atmosphere for teachers.

The goal is to leave no stone unturned. Before hopping on the "T" subway to see the day's schools, Walsh asks a few BES Fellows to give their elevator speeches about the schools they aim to found. These are critiqued too. Walsh listens to a passionate pitch about north Baton Rouge, Louisiana, where 80 percent of children are reading two or more grade levels behind, and the fellow argues for a school where "college starts in kindergarten."

She appreciates the passion, but dislikes the delivery. "When they're your stock phrases you want to own them cold," she says. "You use 'sort of' as a phrase that you should replace with a pregnant pause." Public speaking is part of leadership, and if potential school leaders are trying to convince charter authorizers or parents to give their ideas a shot, their vision needs to grab people.

These fellows wind up at BES for many reasons. Elsie Urueta's family moved from Mexico to Oklahoma when she was a child. Of the Latino students in her high school, she recalls, only she and her brothers went to college. "There are no high-performing non-selective high schools in Tulsa. That's not OK," she says. She came to BES to figure out how to start a school for grades 5-12 called the Tulsa Honor Academy.

Anna Carlstone graduated from UCLA and spent five years teaching English at Junior High School 117 in the South Bronx. She did what she could with her seventh and eighth graders, but "it became extremely frustrating knowing that teachers were hired and brought in in an extremely haphazard way," she says. Her principal was good at keeping people content, but "she was not about to rock the boat. If you said 'your school needs to improve or it will shut down'—she didn't know how. She only knew how to maintain what it had been."

Carlstone wound up at Harvard Divinity School, but while there she learned about several high-performing charter schools including Edward Brooke (another Boston-area school with great results) and Excel. She decided that "the leader is the primary person who makes a difference in the building. The leader's eyes are trained to what an excellent school looks like." She decided to become such a leader, and enrolled at BES to figure out how to start a school in Los Angeles like Edward Brooke.

Walsh justifies the intensity of the training that BES offers by saying "there are 17,000 children in this room." The 17 adults looking to lead schools will each have the power to influence 1,000 children. That's 17,000 opportunities every year to redirect a life.

There are only about 100,000 principals in the U.S. Ensuring that a higher proportion of them have the skills necessary can be an effective way to invest philanthropic dollars.

Many funders come to this same realization. The unit of real change in education is the individual school. That's especially true for charter schools, where the educators in each building have power to make things happen. But even in districts, the school leader has some latitude to set the culture, institute systems to monitor student learning, show up in classrooms frequently, and encourage teachers to work together. Even asking "who are our best substitute teachers, and is learning continuing under their direction?" can give a boost to student gains.

There are 50 million schoolchildren and 3 million teachers in the U.S. But there are only about 100,000 principals. Ensuring that a higher proportion of them have the skills necessary to improve teacher quality and create a culture of learning can be a highly effective way to invest philanthropic dollars. "You could put them all in the University of Texas football stadium," notes Kerri Briggs, former director of education reform at the George W. Bush Institute. "It's a huge lever point."

Management of any organization is not easy. One study by talent managers Development Dimensions International found that people promoted into their first line-management position found the transition as stressful as divorce. So it's good news that organizations and funders are putting fresh emphasis on helping school leaders rise to their challenges.

Who should lead?

The first question to consider when trying to raise principal quality is, as with teaching, how to bring new talent into the field. Very often, "the work conditions that would attract enough of the right people don't exist in education," says Rosemary Perlmeter, co-founder of Teaching Trust, a nonprofit that operates several programs to improve educational leadership. "People who have a deep set of skills and who are highly talented in leading complex organizations usually have a lot of oppor-tunities." In her former Fortune 500 life, "We could pay for top talent."

The obstacles are not just pay. Principals are compensated pretty well. The bigger hurdles may be answering to multiple interests and being in the public eye in ways that corporate managers generally are not. Schools require people who are not only talented but also patient in the face of frustration.

Who exactly are the best candidates for school leadership? In teach-ing, reformers often look to bring in non-traditional sorts. Some argue that this would be a good approach for school leadership, too. Very often, teaching is the only other experience traditional principals have had.

Frederick Hess argues in his 2013 book, *Cage-Busting Leadership*, that this does not serve the cause of school reform. "Those from outside K-12 may find it easier to see that the emperor has no clothes or challenge orthodoxy by asking, 'Why do we do it this way?'."

Because so few traditional principals have outside experience, basic business productivity principles tend to be completely ignored in education. For instance, a lot of research finds that managers can best supervise about 6-9 employees. Yet principals routinely try to closely supervise dozens of teachers, a fact that may be setting up organizations for mediocre performance.

"It's true that there are things about schooling that are unique," writes Hess. "Of course, the same is true for medicine, engineering, law, agriculture, the armed forces, and manufacturing."

"In healthy industries, there's lots of importation" of ideas, notes Bryan Hassel of Public Impact. "If organizations...need experience they don't have, they bring people in from outside."

Some of the common restrictions on who can be a principal make little sense. A few states require that principals teach for a certain number of years in that state. It seems unlikely that the children of different states are so different that a teacher with experience in one state would flounder in another.

Effective teaching experience does seem to be valuable in forming principals, however. Building Excellent Schools doesn't require it, but Linda Brown reports that of the more than 60 schools started by her fellows, "probably two have been led by people with no teaching background." An ideal mix would be a school leader who has done something else in management, but also gotten chalk on her hands.

Jocelyn Foulke at Excel Academy in Boston has plenty of chalk on her hands. A former math teacher and now the head of a school, she regularly puts herself in front of students. "It's a time when I get to teach and share with teachers in the room what I think good teaching looks like," she says. She calls on students without warning, explains, and draws out lessons. She models for teachers how one can make small moments count.

So knowledge of teaching matters. But so do leadership skills and hard-nosed operational wisdom. Anne Stoehr, a former program officer at the Walton Family Foundation, explains that her foundation wants to see "more of an entrepreneurial mindset" when it comes to training principals. The grantees they seek out "are starting to combine more business type skills and leadership skills" with instructional and academic experience. Walton also keeps an eagle eye for "minority talent, and really trying to make sure we're encouraging all of our grantees to be looking out for talent that looks like the students they're serving."

While in the past, people might have moved into leadership roles after a decade or more of teaching, the consensus now is that the ideal candidate will have many interests and skills beyond teaching that will leave him or her ready to move to a principal role after roughly three years of teaching. That experience followed by intense training of the sort now offered by BES and many other leadership academies is producing the sorts of leaders that many school districts are excited to hire.

The residency model

So how exactly do you prepare a good candidate in order to produce someone who can really bring out the best from their teachers and students? Hands-on residencies (which have long worked to train physicians) are a favorite technique today for minting good principals. After its initial training, BES places its fellows into residencies at high-performing schools where they work side-by-side with successful leaders who can show them how to run a school. That same approach of placing prospective leaders under the tutelage of skilled principals around the country, so they can both study their methods and practice leading themselves, is used by the successful trainer New Leaders.

LaToya Caesar worked in the New York schools for several years before joining New Leaders. She currently is a resident principal at West Charlotte High School in North Carolina. This particular school was almost shut down after posting some of the worst results in the whole Charlotte school district in 2006-2007. Fully 90 percent of its students qualify for subsidized school lunch. It's a demographic Caesar knows well. Her parents immigrated from the West Indies, and "I grew up in a very violent, high-crime area in Brooklyn. It was not strange for me to go to sleep to the sound of gun shots."

She was lucky in many ways. "My parents worked hard to make sure I didn't become another statistic. They pushed education. School has been my safe place—where I could completely be myself, and I was encouraged to be the best," she says. "I wanted to do that for someone else."

"As much as I loved teaching," Caesar says, "the way to really create change is to lead and inspire from the top. People gravitate toward inspirational leaders. If you have a vision, and it's a strong one, and you are strategic in the types of people you hire," you can change a school, she believes.

What drew her to New Leaders were the practical aspects of her training. "Much of my graduate-school work was about theory," she says, laughing. "It was theorizing on theory. Here in this program, you are immersed in a really hands-on experience from day one."

New Leaders has taught her a lot about using data to drive student achievement. Now she's applying her new knowledge during her residency in a school where things are starting to work for the first time. The school uses blended learning, one-on-one instruction, and other strategies, and the graduation rate is rising.

"I want to spend 80 percent of my day inside classrooms," says Caesar. "I want teachers to see me, to watch them instruct, to give them feedback." She spends time analyzing each teacher's data, and then has conversations with them on "what we can do to adjust instructionally day to day to make sure all our students are learning."

New Leaders receives funding from scores of philanthropists. In the latest year this includes gifts of a half million dollars or more from Boeing, the Noyce Foundation, the Robertson Foundation, the Carnegie Corporation, the Hyde Family Foundations, and Linnea and George Roberts.

While the residency model has many advantages, it's also fairly expensive—often well into six figures per candidate per year. By comparison, it is possible for funders to start up a new charter school for roughly $500,000 in many places. The Broad Foundation has scaled back its investment in this work partly because of concerns about the gains achieved compared with the cost. Broad was also responding to its finding that principals placed in district schools did less well than those placed in charter schools.

Other organizations, however, have seized on the promise of the residency model that New Leaders, BES, and others use. The Accelerate Institute has created a Ryan Fellowship that provides a year of training not only to future public school principals but also to candidates who want to be leaders in private or Catholic schools. Donors to private, Catholic, and other religious schools may want to consider what an even more far-reaching effort to systematically train successful school leaders for these institutions might look like.

The MBA model

The Rice Education Entrepreneurship Program is an unusual approach to principal training. For a start, it is housed not in a school of education but at Rice University's Jones Graduate School of Management MBA program. REEP aims to train education leaders in business practices as well as educational ones.

Leo Linbeck III, the Houston businessman and philanthropist who helped create REEP, noticed a decade ago that "Houston had quite a bit of growth in the charter sector." High-quality charter networks YES Prep, KIPP Schools, and Harmony were all birthed in the city, and each has expanded rapidly. "What was really noticeable about those programs, and the way they organized their schools, is that they were very leader-centric. There was always a star principal who was making the school a success, largely by attracting and retaining really high teacher talent, setting a cultural context for the school, and keeping the trains running on time."

The question Linbeck and others asked was this: Where would the mushrooming charter sector get more of such leaders? And how could such leaders be injected into traditional school districts? Meanwhile, Rice University, which does not have a school of education, was showing interest in making an educational impact. Interested parties decided that the business school could make a good fit for a different sort of school-leader training program.

"The school leader job is more like running an organization in the business world" than teaching, argues Linbeck. They try to improve results in an environment of constrained costs. They coax the best team performance out of individual contributors. Those are leadership skills of the sort that MBA programs have long taught. Thus was REEP born.

REEP students must be admitted to Rice's MBA program on standard MBA metrics. Once in, they study business practices generally. They also participate in a summer institute that focuses exclusively on educational matters.

REEP graduates often have clear paths into school leadership. One recently became the youngest principal serving in the Houston Independent School District. While the traditional thinking has been that "it might be an eight-year path in teaching to become an assistant prin-

In high-quality schools, there was always a star principal who was making the school a success, largely by attracting teacher talent, setting a cultural context for the school.

cipal, a 10-year path to become a principal," REEP executive director Andrea Hodge says that "we see that shortened, cut significantly" because of the broad skills that her program is able to embed in participants.

REEP isn't cheap. It is heavily subsidized by Houston-area philanthropies, and students pay a small portion of the costs. They can further have their loans forgiven if they work in the area after graduation.

People pay dearly for traditional MBAs that help them land corporate management jobs. While principalships may not have the same financial rewards as some business jobs, the salary doesn't compare badly with a mid-level executive role at a company. Now that REEP has proven the principle, there's reason to think that in the long run education MBAs could attract customers paying much of the freight themselves.

Asked if REEP could be replicated in other places, and with less philanthropic subsidy, Hodge suggests yes. "While I value our Rice faculty tremendously, you can get a good exposure to business skills pretty easily," she says. The key would be to replicate (or piggyback on) the intensive education instruction that REEP has glued onto the normal MBA course. Other universities would need to create their own versions of this—or perhaps send students to Rice's summer institute, or have them participate virtually via online connections.

Hodge says there have been benefits from exposing other MBA students to peers headed into education. "Having a mix of interests creates a different kind of learning environment. It exposes a broader population across Houston to what's happening in education."

While REEP's format is unique, the Lynch Foundation has also worked with a business school to create a principal development program. After surveying the district, charter, and Catholic schools serving Boston children, says executive director Katie Everett, the Lynch Foundation concluded that "a lot of school leaders had extraordinary knowledge of content, and great instructional leadership, but lacked management, budget, marketing, recruitment, and HR skills." Originally intending to set up a program for training principals within Boston College's school of education, the foundation discovered the school of management was a better fit for providing the resources and expertise needed.

BC's Carroll School of Management taught all of the skills the school leaders desired to learn, less the instructional, ideological course work they had already obtained through traditional licensure programs. The Lynch Leadership Academy now resides under Carroll's wing. Aspiring principals and sitting principals who participate in its training get a large dose of training in essential entrepreneurial skills. They also undergo lots of coaching, get a detailed analysis of their own schools, and work under a mentor principal for a year, following the residency model of intensive practical training.

In-house principal training

There's no reason principal training has to happen in an academic institution. Referring to the Lynch Leadership Academy, Katie Everett says "there are many obstacles that make innovation challenging on college and university campuses" versus a program existing on its own. Donors interested in supporting similar training could consider creating a freestanding organization.

Many states are now quite willing to certify alternative programs for licensing principals. There's recognition that much of the principal training at conventional schools of education can be empty paper chasing, and even in the business world there is growing resistance to the idea of sending your young talent off to a graduate school when more hard-headed and immediately useful training can often be offered in house. A number of manufacturers and investment banks, for instance, have stopped automatically supporting MBA studies by their employees, creating systems to train their own leaders in field-tested ways instead.

Unfortunately most school districts lack sensible methods for selecting and developing principals. "Most have insanely bad systems—or no systems. They are crazily unsystematic," says Bryan Hassel of Public Impact. Principal training goes to "whomever raises their hands. I'm exaggerating a little, but not much."

Some charter networks, on the other hand, have leader development down to a science. KIPP is known for its management pipeline. Susan Schaeffler, the CEO of KIPP D.C., says that "in the charter sector, getting good school leaders is the difference between making it and not making it. A bad principal in a charter school is like a migraine." The bad effects of poor leaders are also debilitating at conventional district schools, but in a different way. With their multiple thick layers of bureaucracy, "in a district school, a subpar principal is like a dull headache that goes on forever," she suggests.

At KIPP, all aspiring principals must first prove themselves as teachers. "We want to make sure our principals can go into any classroom, and provide instructional feedback to our best teachers and teachers who are new to the field," says Schaeffler. "We are challenging our best teachers to take it to even another level."

To find educators with the potential to lead, "We look at all of our staff, and we ask who are the next vice principals? Who's five years out, who's two years out? Who are we going to lose if we don't challenge them? Where are our next leaders? Usually it's someone who's a grade-level chairman, who ran Saturday school, who taught tested subjects with strong results."

KIPP schools focus on helping their kids get high test scores along with other concrete markers of achievement, so anyone who wants to be in leadership needs to know what it takes to achieve that kind of show-me proof of success. Like a company that draws its leaders from managers who've shown profit and loss success, KIPP wants leaders who have stood up to benchmarked standards.

KIPP tells principal candidates, "go and teach reading. Go into the high-stakes subject. That is the perfect candidate—one who's taught in tested subjects. Because that's who they're going to be telling what to do when they're coaching, and if they can't do that, they're a little less credible," says Schaeffler. "We want all teachers to look at the administrators and say 'they're amazing.' Those are the kinds of people I want to go to and ask for help or feedback."

> KIPP schools focus on helping their kids get high test scores, so anyone who wants to be in leadership there needs to know what it takes to achieve that kind of proof of success.

Once KIPP has identified such potential leaders, training is built into the career trajectory. KIPP has very specific internal programs—the Fisher Fellowship, and the Miles Family Fellowship, both philanthropically funded—to introduce educators to the KIPP leadership style, and train them to launch new KIPP schools. KIPP regions and schools train their own prospective leaders too.

Schools have two vice principals, so there are plenty of spots to fill. "If you can't afford a two vice principal model, you probably shouldn't open any more schools," suggests Schaeffler. She calls this model "critical to sustainability and long-term success. Some teacher's going to get pneumonia, or not going to show up after Christmas. You can't predict what it is, but if somebody jumps ship, two people can pick up some of the load." This also means that KIPP has less need for substitute teachers, who can quickly dissipate learning gains.

Having two vice principals means that the promotion from vice principal to principal is less stressful. When this happens in a school with a single vice principal, the entire leadership changes over. The new leader has to work with a newly promoted deputy (who's filling her old spot). With two vice principals, the deputy is someone who's been there for a while. For funders who are underwriting school startups, and looking to help schools build their internal leadership capacity, helping to fund a second administrative position "is probably the best money you can spend," argues Schaeffler.

A number of the national and regional teacher-training organizations also now train principals. TFA, for instance, trains principals in some of the districts where it operates. One of the reasons Mind Trust wanted to bring TFA to Indianapolis is that TFA pledged to train new principals there as well—about 5-7 per year currently. The national organization is also scaling up its alumni network to support corps members who are going into school leadership.

The Relay Graduate School of Education also recently started a pilot program for training principals, based on the same practical foundation as its teacher program. Its first corps of school leaders came from both district and charter schools. These leaders learned from Doug Lemov, KIPP co-founder David Levin, and others over the summer. Lisa Daggs of the Fisher Fund visited and reports that "It was just incredibly practical and hands on. All the school leaders I talked to felt like they could take the tools they were given and apply them to their schools the next week."

"I was really struck by the amount of time spent practicing—role playing and getting feedback and doing it over again," she says. To date, much of the successful school leadership at high-performing charters has been "superstar types," but "there's only so many of them out there. As the movement continues to grow, how do we provide the development and support to broaden the pool of leaders?" To the Fisher Fund, Relay appears to provide one good answer, so they have made an investment in its leadership program.

Another option for funders is to encourage a charter network that runs an excellent principal training program to open it up to other schools. Julie Maier of the Charter School Growth Fund reports that her organization is looking at this idea. The high-performing Achievement First network of charter schools is already doing this—helping train principals for three school districts in Connecticut within which it operates schools. The aspiring principals spend half the year at an Achievement First charter school, and half in a district school. "We feel like it's part of our mission," says Paige MacLean of Achievement First. "All children deserve access to great education. So how do we take what we've learned and share it with other people?"

What about boosting the skills of principals already on the job?

Finding and training new leaders is expensive, but it's a long-term strategy that can bear fruit for decades to come. In the meantime, though, there are roughly 100,000 principals already on the job, some of them floundering. Children in the schools these principals lead deserve a sense of urgency about their educations too.

"While it's incredibly important to bring new people into the profession, in the short to mid term we also need to skill up the existing principals," says Jean Desravines of New Leaders. "There is a large set of principals who have the will but not the skill. They believe that all kids can learn at a high level, they just have not been trained to drive teacher practice and drive student achievement gains."

New Leaders has recently set a goal to train 1,000 sitting principals every year. While it operates on a national level, locally focused philanthropies could do the same thing in their region on a smaller scale. Funders might partner with a high-performing charter network or a reform-oriented district to bring in experts who could elevate the competence of sitting principals.

Would sitting principals make time for such self-improvement? They would if there were tougher licensure requirements. A number of states require periodic relicensing for principals, but according to the Bush Institute, almost no one ties principal licensure to school performance and professional evaluations. This is an area ripe for reform. "You have to use test scores as a measurement of student outcomes. That has to be a key part of how you hold principals accountable," urges Desravines of New Leaders.

If principals needed to show academic progress to maintain their licenses, there would be increased interest among them in learning new effective techniques. Maggie Runyan-Shefa of New Schools for New Orleans says she's seen "principals who know things aren't working, but they can't identify what is the problem and prioritize what needs to be fixed." Training run by organizations with documented results might get people's attention in an environment where licensure is linked to results.

Thinking bigger—toward systems that work

The Broad Foundation's discovery, mentioned earlier, that well-trained principals placed in charter schools did better than those placed in district schools is instructive. While the crucial unit in education is the individual schoolhouse, it matters a great deal what kind of system the school floats within. That's why a few organizations are now training leaders for positions above the principal level.

The Broad Foundation, for instance, funds the Broad Residency in Urban Education, which trains managers from other walks of life to work in either a school district headquarters or the leadership of a charter school network. These residents might have an expertise in HR, finance, or some other specialized area. The aim is to improve upper hierarchies that can make conditions better for individual schools. Broad also funds a Superintendents Academy with similar goals. The academy's curriculum was recently revamped and the size of the enrolled cohorts was reduced, to make sure that each prospective leader coming out gets intense training in running and reforming bureaucratic systems.

Ed Pioneers works in 18 cities, including Sacramento, Seattle, and Dallas, to prepare people from top graduate schools and private-sector employers for leadership positions in charter school networks or public school districts. After their fellowships, 70 percent of the participants wind up working in education full time. Funders include the Doris and Donald Fisher Fund, the Broad Foundation, and others.

The Noyce Foundation is likewise funding a residency for administrators headed into large educational hierarchies. It promises practical training for leaders who want to transform education on a large-systems level, and takes place at Harvard's Graduate School of Education.

If good principals are the ones responsible for recruiting, hiring, and coaching great teachers, it's leaders at the next level up who are responsible for shaping the principal corps. So, in theory at least, reform at this level could also prove important. Education is an ecosystem, and it works best when all parts are competent and focused on the same shared principles.

Levers for change

Much has happened in the past two decades to make better educational achievement possible. Reforms generally fall into the categories of "school choice" and "accountability," with these two often going hand-in-hand as new schools publicly hold themselves to higher standards. Not all schools of choice are great. A significant portion, however, are much better than the average district school.

In places where high-performing charter schools have been encouraged to thrive, effective schools have become common even in poor neighborhoods. People see what it actually takes to organize a great school, and reforms spread. The first generation of high-performing charter schools showed that with hard work and great teaching, children from disadvantaged backgrounds can achieve at high levels. The replication of some of these schools has shown they are not flukes.

Ideally, these demonstrations that change is possible would inspire everyone in education to buckle down and do whatever it is that effective schools are doing. But there are structural barriers in public education today that obstruct movement toward better teaching and school leadership:

- Under many union agreements, removing underperforming teachers is an expensive and time-consuming process. For years, districts ran the numbers and figured it wasn't worth the fight, so ineffective teachers were just passed around among schools.
- Under these same agreements, teachers can't be paid different amounts for taking harder jobs or performing better. (For three views on how education reformers might handle teacher unions today, see the sidebar on page 77.)
- Teachers are often laid off during "reduction in force" periods based on seniority alone, known as LIFO (last in, first out). This limits a principal's ability to keep her best talent, regardless of when they were hired.
- As states consider incorporating student achievement into teacher evaluations, resistance is enormous (this was at the heart of the Chicago teacher's strike that delayed school opening in 2012). Where pay differentials based on performance get considered they are often small compared to the old systems built solely on years of experience and education degrees attained.
- Today's strict limits on class sizes, the last generation's favorite school improvement trend, force schools to hire more teachers than they otherwise would. There isn't an inexhaustible supply of good teachers, so smaller classes force schools to dip deeper into the barrel than they might wish.
- Strict licensure systems require a lot of coursework—but not a lot of practical training—and turn talented people away from trying education as a second career.

- Principals don't have as much say in hiring as managers do in other industries. Great organizations first get staffing right. It's hard to go anywhere if you're stuck with staff you can't select or change.
- While education in general isn't short on cash (the U.S. spends significantly more on K–12 education than any other nation), astonishing chunks of it go to bureaucracy, rather than teacher excellence.
- Promotion to leadership positions isn't as thoughtful as it could be. Some people go into administration not out of desire to improve schools, but because they're burnt out from being in the classroom, or want to make more money.
- Principal training often lacks focus on instructional leadership and hard-nosed operational discipline, the two most important skills of school management.
- School schedules, paperwork, and administrative requirements often eat into teachers' planning time, and discourage teacher collaboration and creativity.
- Caps on charter school numbers or enrollment prevent more rapid expansion of some of America's highest-performing and most innovative schools.
- Hesitancy to use technology in new ways, like larger classes for great teachers, means that the best instructors reach far fewer students than they could.

With brave leadership some of these barriers to good teaching and principal work may be less daunting than they seem. People often don't try things just because no one ever has. In 2008, Rick Hess and Coby Loup analyzed union agreements and personnel policies in the 50 largest school districts, and found that "the majority included room to maneuver. While one third of the contract provisions examined were clearly restrictive, half were ambiguous or silent when it came to key questions—and 15 percent offered explicit flexibility to school and system leaders."

Inventive, courageous school leaders can sometimes find ways around problems even in sclerotic districts. A superintendent may inform principals who rate all their teachers as superior (when the results show no such thing) that they're going to have more ineffective teachers transferred into their school because they seemingly have more than their

More than 80 percent of teachers belong to one of the two major teacher unions, and detailed union agreements control procedures in most districts. Below, three experts offer contrasting ideas on how education reformers should cope with the enormous influence of teacher unions.

What to do with unions? Work with them

By Andrew Rotherham

Unions often resist serious reforms of the teaching profession. This is hardly surprising. Membership organizations have a built-in bias towards addressing the present-day concerns of their constituents rather than securing benefits for their industry overall. But teacher unions will continue to be a fixture on the education landscape, which is why some grantmakers are supporting reformers within union ranks and seeking ideas that unions can embrace.

This can be easier said than done. Dan Katzir of the Broad Foundation notes that reform-minded union leaders have frequently been "tossed out of office because they were trying to do things differently."

Phillip Gonring of the Rose Community Foundation recalls that Denver's groundbreaking pay-for-performance initiative was "brutal on union leadership. It was essential to build political support for them."

Potential areas where union reformers might be cultivated include changing teacher contracts to better reflect school-improvement goals, experimenting with alternative compensation schemes, and developing fresh roles for union involvement, like teacher preparation, mentoring, and evaluation. Grantmakers should harbor no illusions about the difficulties involved in dealing with teachers' unions. To date, results have been scant and donors have often been frustrated. Unions, though, are not going away, so donors should build partnerships where possible.

—Andrew Rotherham is co-founder of Bellwether Education.

What to do with unions? Work around them

By Rick Hess

Promoting teacher and principal excellence by collaborating with unions is at best an uncertain strategy. When possible, donors would do well to work around the unions. Here are three strategies for doing so.

Support alternative professional organizations. In right-to-work states, where educators have the right to decide for themselves if they want to join a union, many teachers sign up for the safeguards like liability insurance and legal assistance that membership provides. Donors should consider supporting alternative, professional, non-union groups that provide such benefits. The Association of American Educators is one such organization, providing teachers with the key benefits of union membership, but not at the cost of the unions' anti-reform agendas. Another such organization is the Christian Educators Association International.

Engage with charter schools that suffer far less from union strictures. Charter operators are free to recruit, compensate, deploy, and evaluate teachers in more flexible and intelligent ways. They have birthed new training programs and even graduate schools that attract fresh talent to teaching and bypass stultifying union influences in conventional teacher colleges

Support school systems seeking to change their human resource operations. Some bold superintendents try to reshape their teaching forces by embracing alternative teacher recruitment, training, and licensure

programs. They deserve help.
—Rick Hess is director of education policy studies at the American Enterprise Institute.

What to do with unions? Work against them

By Scott Walter

American K-12 education badly needs change—yet the status quo is powerfully defended by teacher unions. The hope for a "reform unionism" is, education expert Terry Moe says, "a fanciful notion, based on a fatal misconception: that the unions can be counted on not to pursue their own interests." Teacher unions' three sources of power— members, money, and credibility— must be confronted.

Donors can support charter schools, where unions have little sway. They can offer scholarships for low-income children to attend private or religious schools. They can work to secure tax credits and vouchers.

As union membership diminish- es, so too will the tens of millions of dollars per year unions inject into anti-reform politics.

"Paycheck protection" laws can tighten union purse strings by making it easier for teachers—many of whom don't support their unions' politics—to withhold the portion of their dues going to politics. This has been tried in several states and sometimes leads to a dramatic reduction in union political funds.

With media encouragement, the public tends to equate "teacher unions" with "teachers." Reformers must reframe school reform debates and support effective teachers with merit pay, layoff protections, and such, while noting that unions protect incompetents.

—*Scott Walter is vice president at the Capital Research Center.*

share of stars. A principal may set up his office in an incompetent teacher's classroom until she shapes up or resigns of her own accord.

Hess points out in his 2013 book *Cage-Busting Leadership* that school administrators often have options that they choose not to explore or make use of. The same could be said of donors who are eager to change bad policies yet don't realize they have alternatives at their disposal—if they will think creatively and provide bold leaders with the backing they need to undertake contentious reforms.

The $60 million that philanthropists offered Washington, D.C., public schools if they would implement a system of assessing and paying teachers according to demonstrated results allowed reformers to get agreement from the Washington Teachers Union. It needn't always require that much money for smart funders to reinforce good leaders. A good principal can do a lot with a modest pool of no-strings-attached funding. She might see that an excellent writing teacher is getting burned out from too much essay grading and hire two English grad students to help.

Beyond directly supporting good leaders in their target regions, here are 16 broader funding strategies that donors can follow to advance the causes of teacher and principal excellence:

Change public policies

Some of the most important school-improvement victories of the past decade have come in the form of policy changes that do away with barriers to improving teacher quality. Funders in a number of states, including Colorado, Tennessee, Illinois, and Indiana have changed destructive laws. For example, donors helped eliminate last in, first out laws, which required that the only criteria for dismissing teachers be date of hire, causing excellent teachers (even teachers of the year) to be discarded instead of persistently low-performing teachers. Donors also helped pass laws to create incentive pay, require meaningful teacher evaluations linked to student outcomes, and change tenure laws (either doing away with tenure altogether, or granting tenure only when teachers have proven themselves consistently successful at raising student achievement).

There are a number of ways that donors can spur policy changes. In cases where districts, teacher unions, and donors agree on reforms, developing and implementing improved policies may be the best role for philanthropy. In more contentious circumstances, donors can support advocacy efforts aimed at improving laws. For foundations, this means

> Policy changes can bring more permanence than reforms simply instituted by brave administrators who may later pass from the scene.

501(c)3 advocacy. Individual donors can back reformers with 501(c)3, 501(c)4, 527 PAC and SuperPac giving, and direct campaign contributions. While some donors may recoil at the idea of political giving, many have found it to be a tool that cannot to be avoided.

Policy changes can bring more permanence than reforms simply instituted by brave administrators (who may later pass from the scene). "Many times in education, a foundation will push for years to get a program or an idea into a district," says Houston philanthropist John Arnold. "And they get it in, and they think that's the big success. A year or two later, the superintendent leaves. A new super comes in, and that program isn't the new guy's work, and it gets swept away. By this time, the foundation is on to its next project. So it spent several years and a lot of money trying to get this program incorporated into the district, but much of the effort can be wasted unless there is proper advocacy and political efforts to gain support within the organization."

A number of top advocacy organizations are dedicated to improving teacher policies, including Democrats for Education Reform, 50CAN, Stand for Children, and StudentsFirst. These groups focus on various states and different issues of interest to donors. Policy change often doesn't come quickly or easily, so patience is required. As StudentsFirst founder Michelle Rhee puts it, "a sustained effort over a five- to ten-year period" is sometimes needed. For deep and lasting change, donors must recognize that advocacy efforts are, "not just situational fights. It's a comprehensive strategy...and you've got to be in for the long haul."[1]

Excellent advocacy organizations that exist in just one state are also worthy of consideration for investment, as these groups often have a clear view of the issues their states face, and a bounty of local relationships. Groups like Advance Illinois and Tennessee's State Collaborative on Reforming Education (SCORE) have made significant progress, often working with state chapters of national advocacy organizations. The Policy Innovators in Education Network, or PIE Net, counts many of these organizations as members, and is a great resource for donors considering state-level action.

Grassroots groups that organize parents and community voices for policy advocacy can be very effective. Groups like Great Oakland Public Schools, for example, help parents improve educational offerings for their children—like a teacher evaluation system in Oakland that "includes multiple measures of good teaching and student growth while emphasizing professional growth and support for teachers." Groups like Families for Excellent Schools that help give parents a voice have proven effective in recent years, because it is much harder for teacher unions and politicians to dismiss parents pushing for better policies.

Teach For America helped develop Leadership for Educational Equity, a group that recruits and offers early support to TFA alumni willing to run for political office. Numerous other groups also work to find and support promising candidates. Individual donors can directly back reformers who run for public office, from gubernatorial races to school board and mayoral candidates. Laura and John Arnold spend a lot on educational charitable work, but they also "support candidates who are willing to stand up against powerful special-interest groups."

Donors can play a major role in local races like those for school board. Progress can come quickly in such venues. The Indianapolis philanthropy Mind Trust and local individual donors helped a number of reform-oriented school board candidates in their city in the November 2012 election. After a very modest investment, voters chose a reformist majority that will make problem-solving much easier.

---

1. For an extended interview with Michelle Rhee on this subject, see philanthropyroundtable.org/topic/k_12_ education/interview_with_michelle_rhee

"I can tell you from personal experience that you get much, much more bang for your buck" when you complement educational philanthropy with political investments, reports Jim Blew, education adviser to the Walton Family Foundation. "It's not twice the impact per dollar. It's an order of magnitude difference per dollar." Betsy DeVos, a longtime proponent of school reform, agrees. "It took me a while to understand that an advocacy and political effort has to go hand-in-glove with the charitable effort," she says. "Ultimately, elected officials make decisions about legislation that can either permit or preclude meaningful educational reform."

Another way donors can address public policies that harm teaching is by supporting litigation. Students Matter, a nonprofit founded by Silicon Valley entrepreneur David Welch, has helped to press a constitutional challenge in California aimed at improving the caliber of teaching in the state's public classrooms. The lawsuit *Vergara v. California* argues that three teacher policies—permanent tenure after only 18 months on the job; dismissal statutes that require an onerous number of processes to dismiss a bad teacher; and requiring layoffs by seniority rather than competence—violate California's constitutional guarantee of every child's equal right to access a quality education.

This constitutional challenge addresses clear needs in California. In the last ten years, only 19 California public school teachers have been dismissed for ineffectiveness.[2] There are about 300,000 teachers in the state.

Fund research on specific problems

Research is a sweet spot for philanthropy. It can be relatively cheap, and if the results are interesting, research can have wide influence.

A few years ago, the Annie E. Casey Foundation contributed about $200,000 to TNTP for a series of reports that included an influential paper on "Missed Opportunities." People once thought that no one wanted to teach in inner-city schools, but TNTP studied four urban school districts and found that they had far more applicants than needed, and attracted strong candidates with credentials in hard-to-staff subjects such as special-ed and secondary math and science. Yet these districts didn't wind up hiring their highest-quality candidates. TNTP traced these missed opportunities to solvable bureaucratic issues and offered solutions.

The Measures of Effective Teaching project funded by the Gates Foundation established in randomized-trial research that certain class-

---

2. studentsmatter.org/our-case/vergara-v-california-case-summary/#sthash.xSWzRAvH.dpuf

room practices do lead to good student outcomes. The Joyce Foundation funded a helpful evaluation of Chicago's REACH system for evaluating teachers. There's been a lot less research on the principal front. "There needs to be a MET-style big research project on leaders," says Bryan Hassel of Public Impact. "Which leaders are moving students and which aren't? Then mapping the results back so those qualities can become the basis for selecting future leaders."

Funders can require research on results when they make new program grants. Don't just fund an intriguing form of teachers training. Attach funds for an independent analysis afterward to see if the technique worked.

Since many districts are plunging into teacher coaching, this field is ripe for creating standards and some sort of measurable results that coaches could be judged on. "Coaching seems a great thing to do, but no one's measuring how effective it is," says Mora Segal of ANet.

The rise of instant assessment technologies could make teaching more science and less art. With better knowledge about what techniques get results, good teachers may be able to become great. Evidence-based teaching analysis holds real promise.

Fund charter schools

When it comes to improved teaching and school leadership, a large portion of today's most productive innovation and discovery is taking place in high-quality charter schools. Opening new charter slots where teachers and principals can experiment and improve in flexible institutions will do wonders for the state of American schooling. But while they are expanding rapidly, charter schools still reach only 6 percent of American children. Funding educational entrepreneurs to start new schools, underwriting the expansion of proven charter networks, donating to a charter school incubator—there are many ways to widen the opportunities for fine teaching by supporting charter schools. See the 2014 Roundtable publication *From Promising to Proven: A Wise Giver's Guide to Expanding on the Success of Charter Schools* for details on navigating this sector.

Fund big ideas

The Common Core, which received early support from philanthropy, is an effort to raise standards across American education. A total of 45 states plus the District of Columbia have pledged to hold themselves to higher standards of curriculum and annual assessment. This demonstrates that there is a role for big and ambitious reforms on donor agendas, in addition to the more bite-sized efforts that contribute to progress.

New ideas don't have to be fully implemented to help advance reform. The Mind Trust in Indianapolis produced a report a few years ago on "Creating Opportunity Schools" that basically called for power and money to be taken away from the central district office and devolved to individual schools. While there was much push back, more than 80 articles were published in the media about the proposal, and it got the city talking about what it wanted its schools to look like. It also provided a starting point for the education platforms that numerous school board members ran for election and won on, yielding a reformist school board majority.

Convening interested parties in your community to formulate new visions can be a productive role for philanthropy. Julie Maier of the Charter School Growth Fund notes that "bringing together people in similar roles, having similar challenges, has proven to be extremely powerful for us." Her organization gives many school leaders the chance to learn from each other, and "when we get these guys in a room together, magic happens."

Work for better teacher licensure policies

Why shouldn't every teacher have to demonstrate good effects on students in order to stay on the job, and certainly to get tenure? Today, says Tim Daly of TNTP, "The levers of certification are completely misaligned to what we know about teacher effectiveness." A funder could encourage states to craft policies that tie teacher licensure (and renewal of licenses) to actual performance as measured by her students' progress during a school year. Daly suggests that instead of teachers passing tests and coursework to get a permanent certificate, beginning instructors should get "some kind of provisional certificate, so you can enter the classroom on a temporary basis, and at the end of the first year, end of the second year, prove yourself." It's best to figure this out early, and remove ineffective teachers before removal becomes a difficult and expensive process.

Some reformers believe that the barriers to entry for teaching should be lower, with principals empowered to hire anyone they consider well-suited to succeed (as long as they can also weed out underperformers as quickly as possible). There are certainly upsides to this approach. If an engineer who's taught college courses on the side for years retires and wants to teach high-school math as a second career, why shouldn't a principal be able to seize that opportunity?

The BASIS school network does exactly this, hiring a large number of career-switchers to instruct classes. Starting charter schools only in locations that are free from the burdens of formal training and licensure requirements, BASIS regularly hires former playwrights, software engineers, diplomats, NASA physicists, archeologists, and the like to teach in areas where they have subject expertise. Few if any of these instructors would qualify for teaching jobs in traditional schools. The evidence bears out this approach. Across their network of public charter schools in Arizona, Texas, and D.C., children attending BASIS schools test among the top 1 percent of students in all developed countries.

As for tenure, many education reformers don't like the idea of granting tenure at all. If it exists, it should certainly be a reward for proven great work. Around 20 states now have policies for looking at student achievement at least somewhat when making teacher tenure decisions. Funders could work with state regulators to strengthen these assessments and link tenure closely to proven ability to lead children to excellent performance.

> BASIS regularly hires former playwrights, software engineers, diplomats, NASA physicists, archeologists, and the like to teach in areas where they have subject expertise.

Help pay teachers more, or at least differently

While under many union contracts there may be no way for a district to pay more for tough assignments or in-demand specialties, potentially a funder could. A creative funder might start fellowship programs that basically extend the ability of teachers to improve student performance, and enrich them for their effort. This is what Math for America has done, offering an additional stipend to talented math and science majors who choose to teach. As part of the fellowship, teachers could meet on some weekends and in the summer for additional training.

Funders might worry about issues of sustainability. If any significant number of teachers are involved, stipends quickly get expensive, and cannot be continued for years on end. They might help, however, as a short-term way of attracting new candidates into teaching who would otherwise be put off by the starting wage. And once needed educators have been paid to do certain things with good results, it may be possible to chip away at resistance to merit- and performance-based pay with public funds. That was the theory behind the deal in Washington, D.C..

Even in the absence of direct compensation, funders could come up with ways of using cash to help retain and motivate great teachers. Philanthropists might fund sabbatical programs and summer studies for high-performing teachers, stipends for science teachers to work in research labs, or performance opportunities for music instructors.

Philanthropists can also fund travel aimed at professional development. A big thing a strong leader does is help teachers understand what "good" looks like. People who've only seen a high school football game would be stunned to see the plays that work on a pro level. Likewise, teachers need to see great teaching, particularly in the context of a supportive wider system. Anna Carlstone, one of the BES fellows starting a school in Los Angeles, says that "I want my staff to observe at Edward Brooke school, the model that informs my vision…. How am I going to get them out to see the best schools?" This might be the sort of thing that targeted philanthropy can enable.

Invest in new teacher and principal training programs

Most prospective teachers study at education schools. You could, of course, work with a school of education to create a program focused on practical skills, rigorous reading instruction, and so forth. There is certainly space here for a brave funder, though many a previous reformer has exhausted himself trying to reorient traditional teacher colleges.

Alternative certification programs are much more promising, but most are small at present. "It's like the early days of the charter movement," says Julie Mikuta of the Schusterman Family Foundation. "They are only going to ever educate a certain portion of the whole student population. We love these alternative programs, and we're going to help them expand, but at the end of the day it's unlikely that schools of education are going to go out of business."

The Relay Graduate School of Education and Match's graduate school of education have shown that effective new programs can be created from scratch. Funders could work with high-performing charter schools in their region to start similar institutes to train and certify teachers for their schools, and also for other schools willing to hire teachers graduating from them. In particular, if these new programs produce significant numbers of good candidates in hard-to-fill specialties like English-language instruction, special-ed, math, and science, demand could be brisk.

Principals likewise need good training. The Rice/Lynch Academy approach of placing an educational leadership program under the wing of a business school could potentially be replicated. Donors may find that business schools are less beholden to traditional educational notions, and able to inspire fresh thinking. Since almost all principals have already spent time in the classroom, it is in the areas of leadership and management where they need help anyway.

Bring alternative teacher providers to your community
Programs like TNTP, Teach for America, and ACE differ in important ways, but they have all succeeded at drawing talented candidates into teaching who would otherwise be unlikely to consider the profession. Significant numbers of alumni from each of them end up staying in education, contributing in other ways if not as a lifelong teacher. Help these groups come to your city and you will not only enjoy an infusion of teaching energy, but also a following echo of principals and educational entrepreneurs.

Create a better teacher-hiring ecosystem
If your community already has TFA, or if you can't afford the significant cost of helping them establish a permanent program in your region, there are other things you can do to change the teacher landscape. One is helping existing local institutions produce more of the kinds of teachers who get results. In many communities, the lion's share of teachers get their degrees from just a few area colleges. A funder could focus on raising standards at these feeder colleges.

Funders might also offer financial incentives that local districts could pass on to their best classroom instructors to encourage them to take on student teachers, so the novices get off on the right foot. Donors might also pay for experts on what great teaching looks like to come to local schools and offer workshops for teachers and principals on what has been proven to work and what has not.

Promote smart uses of technology to enhance teaching
Schools are only beginning to understand how blended learning can make teachers more effective while lowering overall costs (or at least holding them constant). While buying machines is usually not the best role for philanthropy, helping districts understand the latest thinking on uses of education technology can be valuable. Aspects of blended learning can be brought into the classroom, even if the entire process is not

fully adopted by a school. Donors such as the Joyce Foundation are looking for ways to help teachers use regular computerized assessment to get faster and more personalized understanding of student progress, for instance. This could encourage better teaching.

Professional development is certainly an area that could be improved by better use of technology. Online classes and video archives of excellent teaching in action now make it easier for working teachers to learn from the best. TNTP's Great Teaching, Great Feedback project hasn't gotten as much uptake as one might like; there may be ways to better disseminate it. The demand for good learning tools is out there, if funders can figure out ways to expand access and make continual improvement convenient.

Fund prizes for excellence

Many donors feel that the federal government's Race to the Top grant created a considerable amount of change for the comparatively modest sums involved. It encouraged states to link teacher evaluations to student performance, for instance. Prize competitions might be a mechanism funders can use effectively as well. Could you give a big prize for a professional development program that teachers love and find effective? Could you reward a teacher-training program that succeeds at attracting more students who majored in science, technology, engineering, and math into teaching? Could you give a prize for new principals whose schools show the greatest improvements?

Done right, prizes can reward good results while stimulating innovation. Katie Everett of the Lynch Foundation describes the Sontag Prize in Urban Education, now housed within the Lawrence Public Schools of Massachusetts, as an example of a prize with spillover benefits. The district gives a stipend to great teachers from around the country, and then has these educators come teach for a week to small groups of Lawrence students who need extra help. Everett reports that some of these educators have helped students achieve

> School board elections are often decided by very small numbers of votes, and even small contributions can provide much-needed fuel for a reform candidate's campaign.

dramatic gains in that single week. This is not only good for students, but instructive for teachers.

Work with teacher unions

If working with schools of education has been difficult for education reformers, influencing teacher unions might seem like an even more fraught strategy. But there are reasons for funders to try.

For starters, unions have far more clout over education policy today than any other interest. Any change that can win support, or at least tolerance, from teachers unions has a vastly better chance of enactment. There is sometimes room for common ground between reformers and unions on lower-profile issues that don't make headlines. As one example, the NEA put out a 2009 report called "Children of Poverty Deserve Great Teachers" that embraced alternative certification and better teacher evaluation systems as tools for getting great teachers into high-poverty schools. It even went so far as to call dismissing incompetent teachers "necessary" (while arguing that it's hard to fire your way to greatness).

The NEA has thrown its weight behind the Common Core, one of today's most ambitious efforts to raise the standards of teaching and learning. An article on the NEA's website asserts that "the majority of teachers see the new standards as something to get excited about." Many of the comments on this article from NEA members are negative, but its very existence shows that union members don't have uniform opinions.

It may also be possible for funders to cultivate helpful groups of teachers outside of the union structure. The Joyce Foundation and other funders have underwritten independent teacher associations that allow like-minded teachers to gather, formulate ideas, and speak for their profession in the press and policy discussions. For instance, Joyce gave a $175,000 grant in 2012 to start a Chicago chapter of Educators 4 Excellence. TNTP produced a report in early 2013 called "Perspectives of Irreplaceable Teachers," which surveyed over 100 award-winning teachers on what they thought of the profession and various policies. Creating forums for alternative voices to speak for teachers could be useful.

Invest in grassroots advocacy

One of the Achilles heels of education reform is that it has often been driven by charismatic leaders. A strong leader can motivate people to move mountains, but leaders can also become lightning rods, and when they transition on a movement will sometimes lose momentum. How much of the reform legacy of Michael Bloomberg and Joel Klein will endure now that successors with very different ideas have taken over in New York City?

Encouragingly, charter schooling is one element of education reform that is in the process of developing its own grassroots political constituency. In early October 2013, tens of thousands of parents and children benefiting from charter schools marched across Brooklyn Bridge in support of New York's charter-friendly policies. Philanthropists interested in the cause of education reform can support these voices, aid the policy groups that help them develop constructive new ideas, and assist reform minded political candidates when possible. Foundations can't directly support candidates or lobby, but individual donors can. School board elections are often decided by very small numbers of votes, and even small contributions can provide much-needed fuel for a reform candidate's campaign.

Support termination fights

While consensus is nice, sometimes philanthropists should help advocates for excellent teaching fight in courts and by other available means to make sure there are consequences for failing children. The sheer volume of rigamarole necessary to fire a tenured teacher for incompetence has often led districts to leave even abysmal teachers in place. It costs the Los Angeles Unified School District an average of $238,000 and four years of processes and hearings to fire one ineffective teacher. To combat this, donors might back lawsuits like the *Vergara v. California* case described earlier.

Stephen Brill's 2009 *New Yorker* story on the so-called "rubber rooms" where the New York City public schools parked teachers awaiting dismissal hearings horrified people. Deep in the heart of the worst recession since the Great Depression, New York was paying $22 million a year to teachers who would sit in centers and do nothing all day long. From a taxpayer perspective, this is awful, but at least it ensures that incompetent people aren't standing in front of children. A bad teacher can damage thousands of youngsters over the course of a career.

It's usually not impossible to get rid of bad teachers, just extremely time-consuming and expensive. That's something funders might be able to help with. So buyouts—or court cases—might make sense. In Houston, teachers flagged as ineffective were offered buyouts. Most accepted, and the ones who didn't were put into substitute teaching roles.

Philanthropists might pay for outside legal assistance to advise districts how best to fight policies that would otherwise keep bad teachers in the classroom. They also could pay for outside staffing to tackle administrative burdens of creating reports on teachers who need to be terminated, so the paperwork doesn't take too much time and energy away from the running of a school.

Shape the conversation

Stories like Brill's, or a movie like Waiting for Superman can help crystallize problems in the public mind. Shining spotlights on good teaching, and on bad teaching, can help set up necessary changes in policy and practice.

Among children suffering under poor teachers, talents will often remain like silver in a deep mine: untapped, unrefined, ultimately useless. There's a sign on a wall at the offices of Building Excellent Schools with a single word: Urgency. Improving teacher and principal quality is the centerpiece of raising school quality, and children stuck in the classrooms of ineffective teachers don't have time to wait. A childhood can't be repeated. A child who isn't reading well by midway through elementary school is at great risk of never reaching her potential, and a relay of ineffective teachers can cheat a child out of the chance to be a productive citizen.

A relay of effective teachers led by effective principals, on the other hand, can launch a child into a thriving life. It is hard work, but necessary work if you care about our nation's next generation. Far-sighted private donors, investing wisely, have a better chance of catalyzing the necessary changes than anyone else in America.

INDEX

ABOUT THE PHILANTHROPY ROUNDTABLE

The Philanthropy Roundtable is America's leading network of charitable donors working to strengthen our free society, uphold donor intent, and protect the freedom to give. Our members include individual philanthropists, families, corporations, and private foundations.

Mission
The Philanthropy Roundtable's mission is to foster excellence in philanthropy, to protect philanthropic freedom, to assist donors in achieving their philanthropic intent, and to help donors advance liberty, opportunity, and personal responsibility in America and abroad.

Principles
- Philanthropic freedom is essential to a free society
- A vibrant private sector generates the wealth that makes philanthropy possible
- Voluntary private action offers solutions to many of society's most pressing challenges
- Excellence in philanthropy is measured by results, not by good intentions
- A respect for donor intent is essential to long-term philanthropic success

Services
World-class conferences
The Philanthropy Roundtable connects you with other savvy donors. Held across the nation throughout the year, our meetings assemble grantmakers and experts to develop strategies for excellent local, state, and national giving. You will hear from innovators in K–12 education, economic opportunity, higher education, national security, and other fields. Our Annual Meeting is the Roundtable's flagship event, gathering the nation's most public-spirited and influential

philanthropists for debates, how-to sessions, and discussions on the best ways for private individuals to achieve powerful results through their giving. The Annual Meeting is a stimulating and enjoyable way to meet principled donors seeking the breakthroughs that can solve our nation's greatest challenges.

Breakthrough groups

Our Breakthrough groups—focused program areas—build a critical mass of donors around a topic where dramatic results are within reach. Breakthrough groups become a springboard to help donors achieve lasting effects from their philanthropy. Our specialized staff of experts helps grantmakers invest with care. The Roundtable's K–12 education program is our largest and longest-running Breakthrough group. This network helps donors zero in on today's most promising school reforms. We are the industry-leading convener for philanthropists seeking systemic improvements through competition and parental choice, administrative freedom and accountability, student-centered technology, enhanced teaching and school leadership, and high standards and expectations for students of all backgrounds. We foster productive collaboration among donors of varied ideological perspectives who are united by a devotion to educational excellence.

A powerful voice

The Roundtable's public-policy project, the Alliance for Charitable Reform (ACR), works to advance the principles and preserve the rights of private giving. ACR educates legislators and policymakers about the central role of charitable giving in American life and the crucial importance of protecting philanthropic freedom—the ability of individuals and private organizations to determine how and where to direct their charitable assets. Active in Washington, D.C., and in the states, ACR protects charitable giving, defends the diversity of charitable causes, and battles intrusive government regulation. We believe the capacity of private initiative to address national problems must not be burdened with costly or crippling constraints.

Protection of donor interests

The Philanthropy Roundtable is the leading force in American philanthropy to protect donor intent. Generous givers want assurance that their money will be used for the specific charitable aims and purposes they believe in, not redirected to some other agenda. Unfortunately, donor intent is usually violated in increments, as foundation staff and trustees neglect or misconstrue the founder's values and drift into other purposes. Through education, practical guidance, legislative action, and individual consultation, The Philanthropy Roundtable is active in guarding donor intent. We are happy to advise you on steps you can take to ensure that your mission and goals are protected.

Must-read publications

Philanthropy, the Roundtable's quarterly magazine, is packed with useful and beautifully written real-life stories. It offers practical examples, inspiration, detailed information, history, and clear guidance on the differences between giving that is great and giving that disappoints. We also publish a series of guidebooks that provide detailed information on the very best ways to be effective in particular aspects of philanthropy. These guidebooks are compact, brisk, and readable. Most focus on one particular area of giving—for instance, Catholic schools, support for veterans, anti-poverty programs, technology in education. Real-life examples, hard numbers, the experiences of other donors, recent history, and policy guidance are presented to inform and inspire savvy donors.

Join the Roundtable!

When working with The Philanthropy Roundtable, members are better equipped to achieve long-lasting success with their charitable giving. Your membership in the Roundtable will make you part of a potent network that understands philanthropy and strengthens our free society. Philanthropy Roundtable members range from Forbes 400 individual givers and the largest American foundations to small family foundations and donors just beginning their charitable careers. Our members include:

- Individuals and families
- Private foundations
- Community foundations
- Venture philanthropists
- Corporate giving programs
- Large operating foundations and charities that devote more than half of their budget to external grants

Philanthropists who contribute at least $100,000 annually to charitable causes are eligible to become members of the Roundtable and register for most of our programs. Roundtable events provide you with a solicitation-free environment.

For more information on The Philanthropy Roundtable or to learn about our individual program areas, please call (202) 822-8333 or e-mail main@PhilanthropyRoundtable.org.

ABOUT THE AUTHOR

Laura Vanderkam previously authored *Blended Learning: A Wise Giver's Guide to Supporting Tech-assisted Teaching* for The Philanthropy Round-table. Her writing on economics, education, careers, and technology has appeared in the *Wall Street Journal, Reader's Digest, Scientific American, City Journal,* and other publications. She is the author of *168 Hours: You Have More Time Than You Think* and the *What the Most Successful People Do* series of e-books. She is a member of *USAToday's* board of contributors, and writes the "168 Hours" blog for CBS MoneyWatch. She lives outside Philadelphia with her husband and three children and blogs at LauraVanderkam.com.